IRREGULARLY BOLD

James L. Henderson

IRREGULARLY BOLD

A Study of Bedales School

★

ANDRE DEUTSCH

First published 1978 by
André Deutsch Limited
105 Great Russell Street London WC1

Copyright © 1978 by James L. Henderson
All rights reserved

Printed in Great Britain by
Clarke, Doble & Brendon Ltd Plymouth and London

British Library Cataloguing in Publication Data

Henderson, James L
Irregularly bold.
1. Bedales School—History
I. Title
373.422'74   LF795.P/

ISBN 0-233-97050-9

. . . to those, whose concern for their dear little ones makes them so irregularly bold, that they dare venture to consult their own reason in the education of their children, rather than wholly to rely upon old custom.

JOHN LOCKE,
Some Thoughts concerning Education

Contents

★

Foreword 11

CREATION (1893–1914) 13

1 The Original Impulse 15
2 The Old Bedales 22
3 The New Bedales 31

ACHIEVEMENT (1914–35) 43

4 The Great War and the Twenties 45
5 Towards the Founder's Retirement 69

ADAPTATION (Since 1935) 81

6 Bedales under the Succession 83
7 The Dunhurst Story 100
8 Hand, Heart, Head, Hunch 107

ASSESSMENT 127

9 The Place of Bedales in Education 129

Appendices

I Useful References 149
II School Constitution 150
III Expansion of School Numbers 1936–76 152
   Index 153

List of Plates

★

	facing page
The Staff in 1899	60
A movement class at Steephurst in 1925	61
The Chief	61
The main block (*Press Association*)	92
The Quad (*by courtesy of André Deutsch*)	92
Steephurst (*by courtesy of* The News, *Portsmouth*)	93
The Quad (*by courtesy of André Deutsch*)	93

A*

Foreword

IN THIS BOOK I have tried to identify and describe what has been going on for more than eighty years in and around a unique educational community. Why does it merit attention, not only from professional educationists but from anyone interested in the upbringing of children in the twentieth century? Because it was founded and developed by a man of rare genius, who, caught by the future, demonstrated the practicality of certain educational measures long before their value was at all widely recognized – residential co-education being only one of them. Because it has witnessed to the possibility of conducting a school free from the defects of the traditional English Public School but incorporating many of its virtues. Because it has provided opportunities for several generations of young teachers to serve their apprenticeships in a congenial atmosphere conducive to critical thinking and constructive pedagogical discussion: a number of them have later occupied responsible positions in both the independent and the state sectors of education. Because it has demonstrated with particular brilliance how vital is the cultivation of the aesthetic element in education. Because, finally, it provides evidence of just how far and no further reform can make headway against the prevailing winds of customary educational opinion – I mean in such matters as discipline, morals, curricula and examinations.

According to the Bedalian ethos, boys and girls may grow up learning to discriminate between licence and liberty, to make honest value-judgements without indulging in moralistic posturing, to treasure knowledge without neglecting the ends for which it is acquired, and to pass examinations without making a fetish of them. Not all the pupils all the time of course; like any other school Bedales has had its misfits and misadventures, but what has given the place its special quality, to which the ensuing pages testify, is its consistent blend of the rational and the romantic in educational practice.

'You have undertaken a work,' wrote a former Bedales colleague, 'which is bound to give you much pleasure and is bound to introduce you or re-introduce you to a great host of interesting people, and which is bound to make you the object of criticism from many sides once the book is published, for there will be plenty of people who were actors in various dramas to tell you in what minor points you were misinformed.'

If they are only minor points, I shall be well content because of the delight I have experienced in contacting the many Bedalians, who, by their contributions, have made this book possible. If I have succeeded in catching something of what Bedales has meant to the generations, who, by learning and teaching there, have made it what it is, I shall have begun to repay the debt I owe personally and professionally to what for me was the school of life.

JAMES L. HENDERSON

CREATION
(1893-1914)

*

CHAPTER ONE

The Original Impulse

★

Why did a few parents and teachers begin to question the ways in which their children were being brought up in the last decade of the nineteenth century? The sources of educational innovation and influence are usually much too complex for precise identification, but in the case of Bedales they are clear enough. The school came into existence as a protest against certain features of the traditional English Public School: its curricula, examinations, discipline and morals.* The protesters for the most part came from the ranks of the intelligentsia: among them was a young man named John Haden Badley.

The *Pall Mall Gazette* of 5 October 1892 records how, when interviewed by a reporter, Badley remarked, 'the points on which we faddists want reforms are – in a couple of sentences – the early specialization which exerts its narrowing influence just as much on the modern side as ever it did under the monopoly of Latin Grammar, and the all-pervading atmosphere of individual competition with its machinery of marks and prizes and scholarships.' Whence did this young rebel come? Who was he?

Badley, born in 1865, tells how 'it was thus by mid-Victorian ideas, traditions and ways of life that my childhood was surrounded; and to these, therefore, are owing the main trends of my character and outlook, however modified by subsequent experience.'† His father was a busy, successful doctor in the Midlands, his mother in spite of her invalidism

---

* 'From 1889 to the beginning of the First World War the Progressive movement in education was a middle class movement for middle class children.' (A. C. Stewart, *Progressives and Radicals in English Education 1750–1970.* London: Macmillan, 1970. p. 143.)

† J. H. Badley, *Memories and Reflections.* London: George Allen and Unwin, 1955. p. 12.

a source of much comfort and delight to her children, particularly because of the enjoyment of the classics of English
literature which she was able to communicate to them. Between 1878 and 1884 Badley was educated, first at a Prepara-
tory School near Rugby, then at Rugby School itself. Although
he was not unhappy there and by conventional standards of
academic achievement was a considerable success, his recollection of it in 1958 remained critical:

Our troops fighting in Libya found stencilled everywhere on walls
the Fascist slogan: *credere, ubbedere, combattere* — believe, obey,
fight! With the substitution of the word 'work' for 'fight' this
might well serve for a motto to be inscribed above the entrance
gateway of a Public School of the traditional type. Accept what
is laid down, do what you are told, and put your whole energy
into doing it – is not that a fair summary of the spirit that has
hitherto animated the Public School system? A training of this
kind, based on traditions and setting its mark on the privileged
few to whom it was given, was at once the natural outcome and
the support of a society that took pride in class-distinctions and
was content with an oligarchic form of government. (op. cit. p. 66).

In these few sentences lies the essence of an education and
outlook which Badley set out to challenge but, despite an
intervening period of nearly one hundred years, it is, ironi-
cally enough, on this 'privileged few' that Bedales does in
fact leave its mark. From 1884 to 1888 Badley was at
Cambridge, becoming a scholar of Trinity College and emerg-
ing with a First in the Classical Tripos. Among his other
activities he once entertained Oscar Wilde to breakfast, and
in the course of the meal he made some remark about the
virtue of moderation. 'Ah! Badley,' replied Oscar Wilde,
'nothing is good in moderation. You cannot know the good in
anything until you have torn the heart out of it by excess.'

As a scholar of Trinity going on to a fourth year of study
and with interests in the forward-looking movements of the
day, Badley naturally gravitated towards those a little senior
to himself who had a reputation for progressive ideas. These
included Roger Fry, Goldie Lowes Dickinson and Edmund
Garrett whose sister, Amy, he married in 1893. Later on she
was to contribute to Bedales her own musical gifts and an

indomitable and active concern for the emancipation of women, which led her into the ranks of the Suffragettes.

While still at Trinity, Badley tried his hand briefly at teaching in Adult Education, came under the influence of Edward Carpenter and realized that, 'Hence-forward what I felt to be real and all-important in religion was not, for me, to be found within the doctrinal framework of any Church.' (op. cit. p. 99.) He was away from Cambridge for most of his last summer term, acting in a temporary capacity as Sixth Form Classics Master at Bedford Grammar School. Although drawn towards teaching as a career, he was however becoming steadily more reluctant to practise within the orthodoxy of the Public School system.

The winter and spring of 1888 and 1889 were spent studying and walking in Germany:

I was still dreaming beside the Laacher See – in memory it is always the home of untroubled peace – when a letter from Lowes Dickinson brought the solution of my problem. He wrote that there was a plan afoot to start a new kind of school that should retain what was good in the Public School system, but with a practical rather than academic training, in the setting of a country-life and its interests. Edward Carpenter was keenly interested in this plan, and had been up in Cambridge in quest of some young graduate who would care to take part in putting it in practice. Dickinson had suggested me as likely to welcome the opportunity. If the plan attracted me, he wrote, I had better come back and see the Headmaster, Cecil Reddie, at once, since the intention was to open the new school in the coming Autumn. (op. cit. p. 104.)

In a letter to his father from Germany dated 14 June 1889, the young Badley gave a revealing glimpse of his motivation:

If teaching is to be my work, I think it must be, or must begin, in some such way as this. As I once told you, I have no ambition that would make me desire to become a Headmaster of a Public School even if such a career were possible; but I have the ambition to do what I can in the fullest way, and trying to live and teach others to live (as far as I have power and opportunity) in what I believe to be the best way. I am aware that this will sound to

you presumptuous on my part: but if I am so young as to believe
that some things may be changed for the better, I am also young
enough to be eager to do all I can, and not to be deterred by
finding myself in a minority. Perhaps I shall grow wiser in time;
at least I am willing to buy the experience and pay the full
price for it.

In acknowledging his debt to Edward Carpenter, Badley adds
a further comment: 'One of the things that I learned from
him was that the best and most useful work one can do is
that which springs from one's own personality as outcome of
an inner need. The man, he declared, who is seeking to liberate
himself from what he feels to be intolerable constraints and
soul-destroying conditions thereby does most to liberate
others.' (op. cit. p. 104.)

Forty years later I myself came under the spell of Badley
at Bedales and can confirm entirely the truth of that observation. Indeed, work springing 'from one's own personality as
outcome of an inner need' and the encouraging and practising
of this activity are the essence of Bedales education.

In October 1889 Badley took up his duties at the New
School, Abbotsholme. His admiration for Reddie was considerable, although he was dubious about the educational impli-
cations of the influence of such an extremely autocratic
personality as Reddie's on his pupils. Nevertheless he openly
acknowledged his own indebtedness to him, that of 'an ap-
prentice to a master craftsman'. After two-and-a-half years,
Badley felt the urge to start up a school of his own, where
he could put into practice not only the ideas he had imbibed
at Abbotsholme but others as well to which Reddie was not
sympathetic – chief of them a looser, though still firm, form
of discipline. In fact, at the time of parting, there was something of a rift between the two men: the same educational
institution could not contain two such masterful characters;
each had his own vision of the educational future.

In June 1891 Badley sketched out his ideas in a pamphlet
entitled: *Bedales (Haywards Heath, Sussex). A School for
Boys. Outline of its aims and system.** It is addressed 'to those
whose concern for their dear little ones makes them so

* Cambridge University Press, 1892.

irregularly bold, that they dare venture to consult their own reason in the education of their children, rather than wholly to rely upon old custom.'*

'The aim,' Badley states, 'is greatly to modify without repudiating the English Public School by embodying in the Founder's scheme ideas on which most exponents of the modern scientific view of education are agreed, and to embody these ideas in practical methods suggested by the writer's experience of the New School, Abbotsholme, at which he has been an Assistant Master from its foundation to the present year, and to which he wishes to acknowledge his deep obligation.'

In a few paragraphs he tilts against the inadequacy of reforms attempted hitherto – 'new wine in old bottles' and at early subject specialization, that is, before the age of fifteen. The 'New School' should 'lay a foundation on which any special structure can be placed without fear: not, as in the old style, a mere fragment of impossible culture, incongruous with any practical building above; and not, in what threatens to be the new style, a scamping of the foundation altogether in order to begin building at the top,' a diagnosis which appears strangely pertinent to the 'Great Debate' on education in England of the late 1970s. In a further paragraph on character training, Badley refers to 'that curious relic of the monastic habit of thought which deprives boys, when herded together at school, of that which is one of the healthiest and most effective forces of home life, the presence and direct influence of Women.'

He then touches on physical training and manual work (with a swingeing blow against the mania for athletics), carpentry, market gardening, and the importance of hygienic habits and the virtues of outdoor life. As regards mental training, 'the subject is of little moment compared with the way it is taught. What then is the necessary equipment of civilized life, of every educated human being?' Badley supplies a core curriculum: 'reading, writing, account keeping, correct speech and spelling; elementary knowledge of geography, of the machinery and laws of the State, and of natural laws; elementary training in arithmetic and grammar

* From John Locke, *Some Thoughts concerning Education*, 1692.

are surely the minimum of education to be given to every child that is to lead a really civilized life. And this minimum every well-taught child of average health and powers could have got at twelve years old.' A philosophy that is hopelessly archaic in the post-Newsom age of Comprehensive schools – or dazzlingly avante-garde?

'The first lesson a child must learn,' continues Badley, 'is absolute obedience to authority. Then, by calling reason and affection into play, obedience becomes rational and willing and the learner becomes in some degree a teacher, and can be trusted with a measure of direction.' He steers an uncompromising course between the Scylla of Dotheboys Hall and the Charybdis of Summerhill!

He concludes by quoting Pestalozzi: 'If the religious element does not run through the whole of education, this element will have little influence on the life; it remains formal and isolated.' 'Children,' says Badley finally, 'will come to question whatever is taught them as dogma: but habits of reverence and love for what is noble and beautiful will not drop out of the mind or leave the life empty, without hope or motive. Worship, art, labour, love, these make men's lives.'

The prospectus for 1893 states specifically:

The aim of the school is to give an all-round education to boys who are intending to go on to a Public School up to the age of thirteen or fourteen, or up to a later age to boys whose faculties are better suited for other lines of training; to develop their powers in a healthy and organic manner rather than to achieve immediate examination results; and thus to lay a sound basis for subsequent specialisation in any given direction. With this view, body, mind and character, as subjects for training are regarded as of equal importance. (School Fees £30 a term.)

A suitable house was acquired on the west side of the Lindfield/Lewes Road in Sussex, its name, Bedales, so called presumably because the sixteenth-century tenants of the Manor held their lands then on condition of having to serve as Beadles or parish officers.

'On January 28th, 1893, three boys arrived and our venture was begun.' (op. cit. p. 122.)

Yet in answer to the question put to him by Mrs Stocks

seventy years later, 'in those days did you have some vision of the sort of school you wanted?' Badley replied: 'No, I was entirely at sea, simply knowing that "the traditional Public School" wouldn't do. I wanted to do something better than that, and I didn't quite know what.'*

No clearer pointer than this is needed to indicate that the venture thus begun was to proceed by means of the empirical genius of the founder, which was, however, very deeply and firmly rooted in his 'simply knowing'.

Such a quality of 'simply knowing' is not easily defined, but among those who knew Badley there is agreement on certain of his characteristics. Throughout his life, his physical appearance was striking – sparingly but sturdily built, a mountaineer, athletic, with a noble head. He was shy, often disconcertingly monosyllabic in his utterances, relating far more readily to children than to adults. I remember how at the end of my first term as a young teacher on his staff I went to take leave of him before the holidays. Having received no communication whatever from him during those twelve anxious weeks of my novitiate, I feared I had been found wanting. We shook hands, his eyes beamed benevolently, but the only words that issued from his lips were, 'Nice to have you with us.'

There was a distinctly Puritan streak in him and, although his convictions were passionate, his emotional life seemed to be kept in check almost to the point of repression. His sense of humour was robust rather than sophisticated, the warmth of his personality coming through most clearly in his teaching. As he spoke of Socrates or Jesus, Buddha or Shakespeare, insight and scholarship seemed to kindle within him, and he captivated his listeners, old and young. Badley had a clear view of man's purpose in living, namely to discover and cultivate his spiritual nature: the cardinal point in his educational philosophy was that all children, if properly nourished, can learn to attain a similar realization.

* From a B.B.C. radio interview, 30 January 1963.

CHAPTER TWO

The Old Bedales

★

From January 1893 until the summer of 1900, when in the
world outside Gladstone divided the Liberal Party on Irish
Home Rule, the Dreyfus case reverberated through France, the
Fashoda incident occurred anticipating the division of Europe
into two armed camps, and Mafeking was relieved – an event
duly celebrated by staff and pupils – the small, intimate community of the first, 'old' Bedales was preoccupied with the
task of launching a pioneer effort in education. In addition to
Mr and Mrs Badley, there were Charles Rice, teacher of
science, T. J. Garstang, teacher of mathematics, Winifred
Cobb, part-time teacher and matron, and O. B. Powell. Because
the last, affectionately nicknamed Osbos, was to be Badley's
right-hand man for some forty years, it is fitting that a first
glimpse of the school in embryo should be obtained through
his own searching eyes:

After Uppingham and Cambridge I had drifted into teaching as a
profession and my first job had been on the staff of the Manchester Grammar School, then in the heart of the city and often
so thick in fog that the back benches of classes of forty boys
were invisible. To me and to one or two other rebels on the staff
it seemed that, apart from future Balliol scholars, the bulk of the
800 pupils were just being pushed through a mill calculated to
produce a cheap and reach-me-down education. I cast about to
find some school that might be putting into practice the ideas
Thring had in mind when he founded Uppingham without being
frustrated, as he was, by the medieval layout and traditions of
the Public School. I was taken on to the Bedales staff a term before the school began in order that I might improve my French
and find out what I could of an original method of teaching

language which was then attracting some attention from Monsieur Gouin in Paris.

My first superficial glimpse of the house on Bedales Hill, Lindfield, was on a cold misty December morning, walking up from Haywards Heath after an early crossing to Newhaven. I had first met J. H. B. at Dudley in the summer and had been put off by the plimsolls, old dress trousers, tweed coat and what was then known as a 'cod cap'. [Incidentally Badley's father remarked on learning of Powell's appointment: 'John, you're surely not going to engage that lackadaisical young man?'] Mrs. Badley I had not met before. I was overwhelmed by her insisting on carrying my suitcase upstairs and wanting me to lie down and rest after my journey. The Djibba [the girls' uniform of loose tunic] and the green stained tables and benches struck me as being 'Grosvenor Gallery' and I wondered for a bit if this was really the place for an ordinary Philistine like myself. Before we sat down to breakfast in the hall, I found on the piano Brahms' 'Wie bist du, meine Königin' and was told it belonged to Miss Cobb, on the staff as Housekeeper and pianist who had just gone home [not long afterwards he married her] . . .

Most of my friends and relations had strongly disapproved of my giving up my job at Manchester to join a school that did not yet exist and where the prospects of earning enough to live on were remote. There was certainly something comic in being one of a staff of three men and three women to teach three ill-assorted boys, but we were all strung up to concert pitch and full of faith that, with J. H. B's leadership and inspiration, Bedales was going to be a place where we all could learn by doing and happily teach by being and so revolutionise English education. I had so loathed the piles of notebooks to correct night by night at Manchester and the struggle to instruct and keep in order vast fog-bound classes, that to find that the time-table, instead of being a complicated cast-iron control, was a pleasant sharing out of the days and weeks, gave immense relief. Between the few formal lessons the gaps were filled in with garden work, with making the necessary school equipment, with converting an old country house, its stables, harness rooms and outhouses into a school.

My first conviction of incompetence as a teacher was when J. H. B. came to see how I was dealing with an Early English

History class. I was terrified and asked him to show me and them how it should be done, and I learnt a good deal from that first bit of help. The making of a choir out of three boys of whom only one had any inclination to sing, reinforced by maid-servants who didn't think it was part of their job, was not easy. Every Saturday evening some member of the staff was expected to give a lecture, entertaining if possible. An early one of mine was on bee-keeping. I had never yet kept bees. The first Sunday evening service has left the clearest impression. The two Psalms that without exception for over forty years formed part of the framework of J. H. B's Sunday talks – the reading of Walt Whitman's 'Where the Great City Stands'. The spring and early summer of 1893 were phenomenally fine and certainly enriched the colours of the amateur stage on which that pioneering company were trying out the first act of their play for a very minute audience. . . . I have a memory that consistently refuses to record unpleasant events, of which no doubt there were many.*

In a letter from Badley to Powell, dated 22 June 1965, there is a revealing and generous passage, which throws light on the nature of their partnership:

I hope you realised from the greeting I sent to the Luncheon Party [held to celebrate J. H. B.'s one hundredth birthday], how much I feel that Bedales owes, and has always owed to *you*. People ought always to speak of it as *our* work (yours and Winifred's, as much as Amy's and mine); and I can never adequately thank you for all you did in helping to make it what it was – and is. To Goldie Dickinson in the first place, with all his wisdom and loving kindness, and his introduction first of me to Reddie and then of you to me, I owe an immeasurable debt of thankfulness; and I hope that all who know Bedales know how much it owes to him as well as to its actual Founders.

By the end of the second year of the school's existence there were thirty boy pupils, by the end of the third year forty, and after that numbers grew at the rate of ten a year, while in the autumn of 1898 four girls were admitted, living three-

---

* O. B. Powell, 'First Impressions of Bedales', in *John Haden Badley 1865-1967. Bedales School and its Founder*. Published by the Bedales Society, 1967.

quarters of a mile away at a house called Scaynes Hill under the care of a Mrs Green. How far this start of co-education was due to the chance propinquity of one or two mothers, who were inclined to let their daughters join a small school which from personal inspection they had learnt to respect, how far due to the determination and persistence of Mrs Badley in fostering the Women's Suffrage Movement, and how far to the influence of the Hon. Mrs Franklin, founder of the Parents' National Educational Union, is open to question. In an interview with Mrs Stocks on 30 January 1963 Badley recollected: 'The mother of a boy in the school was so pleased with what it did for him, that she said, "Couldn't you take his sister as well?" We said we would be delighted to, that was just what we wanted, only we had no one who could run the house for the girls. And she said: "Really, if you will allow me to come, I could do so and bring some of my daughter's friends." '

This lady was as good as her word, as can be seen from the following extract of one of her letters to a friend written on 25 October 1898:

My son is at a school here in which I very much believe: and the Headmaster consented gladly to take my little girl as a day pupil also if I could find a few more to be with her. So I have three little girls here, beside my own, and they go every day to school at Bedales to do their lessons with the boys . . . As I am very much interested in co-education, I am glad to make this experiment, and all the staff are doing their utmost to make it a success in every way. Being Scotch, I suppose, you and your family would not be so much shocked as some people are.

'Next term,' Badley announced in the Bedales Record (10, 1897–8; see Appendix 1), 'the house at Scaynes Hill will be given up to Mrs Green and the girls under her care, who will join us in class and as much as may be possible in other things as well. It will seem strange at first no doubt, but that will soon wear off, and we are determined, one and all, to make it work.'

'At first,' wrote Badley, 'their presence made little difference; then, as their numbers grew, questions of treatment arose. "What am I to do," a Prefect asked me, "when they

break the rules? You see, you can't lick a girl!" I answered
that this was just why they were there, and that some other
way of keeping order must be found.'*

One of the 'Shemales', as they were sometimes referred to
by the boys, reports, however: 'We were not welcomed by
the boys, and we thought then and still think now that our
efforts to make it all a success were not appreciated.' It is in
these terms that the start of co-education at Bedales must be
understood. It was not a deliberate challenge to convention,
but rather an impromptu measure. Just because it did not
contradict Badley's general principles, but fitted in with them
naturally, it eventually established itself as an important,
indeed essential, aspect of the residential life at Bedales. An
article in *The Times* on Friday 2 April 1965, after glancing
at what it would be misleading to have characterized as co-
education in earlier times concludes, 'the distinction of being
the first co-educational boarding school must remain, it seems,
with Bedales. It was there that the foundations were laid of an
education which should not be shaped by either the shibboleths
of the smoking room or by the half-truths of the boudoir.'

It is not too difficult to picture those early days, the morn-
ings taken up with lessons, the afternoons with games and
out-door work, the evenings with a rich assortment of social
activities: debates ('that belts are more important than braces'),
a Shakespeare play or a Merry Evening – the latter to become
a permanent feature of Bedales life and consisting of light-
hearted take-offs of characters in and about the school and
the presentation of skits and sketches. Half of *Macbeth* was
produced, with the heath scene painted specially for the
occasion by Roger Fry, and Mr Badley deputizing in the role
of Macduff for Mr Powell who was suffering from a disabled
leg. Apart from such things as bee-keeping, book-binding and
taxidermy, an obviously important feature of school life was
the more formal lecture.

Mr. Garrett gave us a lecture on South Africa and the scene of
the war then going on in Matabeleland, and, as he was able to
bring down a large number of slides and a collection of orna-

---

* J. H. Badley, *A Schoolmaster's Testament*. Oxford: Blackwell, 1927.
p. 59.

ments, weapons and other interesting things belonging to the
chartered trading company, the Imperial Institute and others, it
seemed a pity to keep it all to ourselves. So we hired the Assembly
Rooms at Lindfield, and he gave it there and the school sang
songs in between. It was a great success; over 100 people came,
and when all expenses were paid we were able to give something
for the families of the miners out of work. (*B.R.* 1, Spring Term
1894.)

It was on a book-plate designed by this same Edmund Garrett
that there first appeared what was to become the school
motto : 'Work of Each for Weal of All.'

Mr. Badley began the term's lectures on January 25th with an
account of the events which had lately been going on in Armenia,
America and the Transvaal . . . His [Dr Jameson's] invasion was
a splendid piece of pluck, but it was nevertheless a mistake
which has had serious results. (*B.R.* 6, 1895–6.)

Cold baths, wet runs, so-called because they took place when
it was too wet for normal games, attending to earth closets,
delightful expeditions to the sea at Rustington, and even
'spankings', were part of school life; in the case of the last the
delinquent was simply informed that 'his presence was required in the soup kitchen', a polite euphemism for the place
where Badley would occasionally wield his cane. The spirit of
those first few years is best caught by glancing at reports
drawn up by persons periodically invited by Badley to inspect
the school.

At Christmas we had, for the first time, an outside Examiner to
examine the whole work of the school. Mr. G. L. Dickinson came
down from Cambridge to do so, and his report showed very
clearly the weak points of the work of the school. The spelling,
writing and general form of the written answers are especially
criticised; there is no doubt that there has hitherto been too little
written work, and this must now be altered. (*B.R.* 6, 1895–6.)

In the *Parents' Review* (1900) T. G. Rooper, one of such
Examiners, created the following image, 'however clumsily
carved', of what he observed at Bedales. It is worth quoting
at length because it provides a kind of standard or measuring

rod for comparison with other epochs of the school's
life :

Cannot we imagine a school which shall be designed as an
extension of the family rather than a substitute? Such an institution would aim at a position between the old-fashioned school
and family life. It would be wider than the family circle, but
the masters would not be out of relation with the boys when
not instructing them, nor mere companions in games. The masters
and boys would have common occupations in farm and garden and
workshop, and in expeditions for surveying, science studies, and
practical work and military training. The boys would not be
left too much to themselves, nor subjected to the degrading
espionage of the pitiful peon* of the French schools. In such a
school there will be a place for both sexes, and the brutality of
Tom Brown's Schooldays would be avoided, while the effeminacy
of a smug boarding house will be equally absent. Hard and rough
work out-of-doors would check the growth of squeamishness, and
evening occupations, in the way of music, literature, recitation,
reading, play-acting and the like, will cultivate refinement. We
want nothing soft, and yet nothing brutal or brutish.

We can imagine a school in the country, where hardihood of
life can be cultivated amid fresh air, open windows and cold
water, where life is simple and varied, and the evils of excessive
sub-division of labour are avoided.

We can imagine a school where the masters lead a common life
with the boys, dressed like them for practical activity in the field,
and not in black cloth, gowns or cassocks, working at gardening
or ploughing, directing the boys at work with them; where the
child is not isolated from the society of adults out of lesson time,
and where adults find a real and not a pretence or toy occupation
in utilising the child's force as far as it goes in work which is
useful to the establishment.

We can imagine that time at this school will not divide itself
into sharply cut sections of work and play, hated restraint
followed by lawlessness and relaxation, but rather consist of
inter-change of occupation, contiguous but varied, some lighter,
some severer, some taxing muscle, some brain.

* A sarcastic reference to the non-teaching superintendent in French
classrooms.

We can imagine that in such a school there would be established a collective, corporate life, in which, however juvenile, each member would learn self-reliance and individual responsibility. The life would call out spontaneous activity and not merely depend on drill, hurry, force and uniformity.

In such a school the idea of liberty which grows up in the mind will not be absence of restraint and order, not anarchy, not forced individualism, not disregard of others, not absence of external control, but rather constant consideration of others, and constant adjustment of the relation of self to other people. The virtue that here grows up will not be negative as of those who are good because they are constrained to be good by force external to themselves, but active virtue such as springs from having lived in a society where good lives are led and where a good life has been led thanks to the environment of a well organised community.

No wonder that if this impression of Mr Rooper's was correct the Bedales motto was indeed appropriate.

Justifiable pride at the first signs that the educational experiment was paying off in terms of academic attainment rings through the following paragraph of the *Bedales Record* (8, 1896–7):

Hoffmann's Scholarship at Cambridge is the first public proof that our manner of life and plan of education with its short hours and varied occupations is not a mere fad, well enough in theory, but unable in practical result to hold its own against other schools. No doubt, Scholarships and Examiners' Reports will not entirely dispel the notion that Bedales is a place where the only serious class is digging potatoes and playing football; but at least they will serve to confirm those who have ventured to believe in us hitherto in the assurance that ideas and methods are not always foolish and impracticable because they are new!

So much for the gibe once flung at the school in those early days, 'Bedales? Oh, yes! That's where they drink cocoa and eat brown bread as if it were the Eucharist.'

Already in the 1890s the school was attracting attention outside England: M. Edouard Demolins, who sent his own son as a pupil to Bedales, opened the first of the 'new schools'

in France. 'From India, from America, from Australia, from
Japan have come letters of welcome and encouragement. From
France, from Norway, and now from Russia beyond the
Caucasus have come enquiries showing the keenest interest
in what we are trying to do.' (B.R. 8, 1896–7.) 'But whatever
different lines they take all are signs of a new life, a stirring
of the dry bones of the educational world.' (B.R. 12, 1899–
1900.)

N. Jarintzoff gives a Russian's view of Bedales in this same
issue: 'The behaviour of the boys to each other and to the
girls, their quiet indifference to the stranger, and at the same
time, the good natured and willing conversation into which
they fall when addressed, make one of the brightest impressions.'

One of these visitors from abroad, who strove to set up a
school on the model of Bedales, was a Madame Livitsky from
St Petersburg. Uneasy speculation is aroused as to her ultimate
fate. Yet it is heartening to record how the link with Russia
has been renewed. On a November day in 1977, some fifty
young musicians from the U.S.S.R. visited Bedales and made
music with the present generation of Bedalians – an educational bridge across time and ideology.

CHAPTER THREE

The New Bedales

★

At the turn of the century increased numbers and the threatened termination of the lease of the Lindfield property compelled the community to seek another site. The site chosen was undoubtedly a fine one: an estate of one hundred and fifty acres lying between the town of Petersfield and the village of Steep in the county of Hampshire. To the south it commands magnificent views of the Downs towards Butser and Wardown, while to the north stretch the Hangers from Stoner Hill to the Shoulder of Mutton – glorious in the green of springtime, russet gold just before the leaves begin to fall.

The new school building, designed by the architect G. H. Lupton, had not been completed when sixty-seven boys and seven girls returned from their summer holidays, the latter accommodated in Steephurst, a house on the estate originally constructed in 1716. It and another house, Dunhill, had farms attached to them; the quadrangle (known as 'the Quad') of the main, new buildings was finished on three sides only, the fourth lying open to the north for several months. The impression received of those winter days at the end of 1900 is one of mud, concrete mixing, pioneering work on the land, the finding of water through Badley's use of a water diviner, and almost continuous wet and cold.

Nevertheless, the spirit of enterprise was stronger than ever before, and the 'Chief', as Badley was designated by T. Garstang, issued a renewed manifesto. A few extracts from it provide the flavour of what Badley then had in mind: *

In order to make clear the purpose and meaning of the school, the outline (issued before its commencement) of what we meant

---

* *Bedales School – outline of its aims and system. An essay in education.* Cambridge University Press, 1900.

to do, now, after these years of work, needs re-writing. Not that our aim has changed, or that we have to fall back from any of the positions then taken. On the contrary the aim has widened as it has taken practical shape. But what was then only a purpose, and might be dismissed as a dream, has now been proved practical; and on the eve of further expansion we felt that it was time to attempt afresh some statement of the educational faith that is in us. (p. 1.)

Note the quiet confidence of those sentences, and the use of 'we' rather than 'I'; Badley was an autocrat sufficiently modest always to acknowledge his debt to others.

'The course here laid down is intended for those whose school life need not be prematurely cut short by the claims of wage-earning and who will almost certainly be, in some degree, however small, leaders in after-life.' (p. 8.) A feature here is the realistic acceptance by Badley of the social class limits within which he recognized he had to operate and also the frank acknowledgement of the need, in his judgement, to educate for leadership.

On pages 32 and 33 he refers confidently to 'the gains of having together different ages and different sexes', while on page 52 there is an interesting passage on school morality:

Not all the precautions or sermons in the world will do any good if the springs of motive are not reached. The problem is to control and direct the forces of life, not to repress or merely prevent their misdirection, and in this all rules are secondary things. A school, when the affections are neither exaggerated into unreal sentimentality, nor laughed or frowned out of sight, and so stunted or forced into unwholesome channels, and where gentleness and helpfulness are esteemed as no less needful than courage and pluck, cannot be brought about by mere rules. What we have to see is that all our rules are helps and not hindrances to this end ...

Children will come to question, and often to reject, whatever is taught them as a dogma: but habits of reverence and love for what is noble and beautiful will not drop out of the mind, or leave the life empty, without hope or motive.

In contrast with the doubts and misgivings of today, what is striking here is the calm air of certainty regarding the existence of a generally accepted code of moral behaviour and the lack of doubt regarding the nature of reverence, love, nobility and beauty. There was a mixed Hellenistic – Judaec – Christian assumption that everyone – when it actually came to it – knew what constituted a 'decent chap' and that 'to do the right thing was the right thing to do'.

Another inspection of the school was conducted by H. L. Withers, Professor of Education at Owen's College, Victoria University, Manchester, in 1901. In the course of an appreciative report he wrote:

There is a belief in some quarters that new methods imply indulgence to caprice and wayward impulse, and fail to produce prompt and absolute absorption in the business in hand. It is of great importance that no sort of colour should be given to such statements, which are generally made in defence of obsolete forms of teaching and organisation. The very reverse ought to be the case. The enhanced vitality produced by life at such a school as Bedales must mean increased powers of self-control.

In 1902 Bedales School received official recognition by the then Board of Education: from 1 August 1911 it was to be included in the Board's List of Efficient Secondary Schools. The report issued after that first official inspection of 1902 concludes:

It appears from the Reports of the Inspectors that an interesting, if not unique, educational experiment is being tried at Bedales School under personal and local conditions so favourable as to suggest caution in accepting the results as of general application. Whatever may be the ultimate outcome of the experiment it cannot but be an advantage in itself that individual educationalists of originality and practical utility should freely submit to the test of public opinion fresh methods and principles adopted with deliberation and carried out with thoroughness.

Reports on the school made by individual examiners in 1906–7 and then in 1908–9, by which time there were one hundred and four boys and fifty-three girls, may be added as further, external evidence. Introducing the former examiner, Badley wrote:

B

As the number of girls at Bedales has been steadily growing, and the school has become more truly co-educational, we have felt that it would be well henceforward to arrange for the annual inspection to be carried out by men and women alternately in order to ensure not only that the interests and needs of the girls are duly considered, but also that the whole scheme of education pursued at the school may not be regarded only from one point of view.

The examiner, Elizabeth P. Hughes, commented:

Perhaps one of the best points about Bedales is the fact that while it does some things that very few other schools attempt, it does thoroughly well what other good schools do. The educational importance of different schools to outsiders obviously varies considerably. Bedales is introducing something new, and its educational importance extends far beyond those who are enrolled as its pupils.

What were some of those new things? How was the school extending its importance? Answers include boarding school co-education, greater emphasis on arts and crafts, escape from negatively-imposed classical studies, postponement of specialization, stronger emphasis on health education, and the influence, even then beginning to spread, of school staff who went on to teach elsewhere and took with them the inspiration they received while at Bedales.

In the 1908-9 report the examiners, Miss Caroline Herford, Miss Janet Cox and Miss E. Needham, wrote:

Those who have had opportunities of trying to fathom the depths of British prejudice in all questions of educational reform are the most likely to appreciate the remarkable work which is being done at Bedales School . . . Bedales is the creation of its great Headmaster. Mr. Badley is an idealist, and he possesses a power of organisation and grasp of practical details, the absence of which so often wrecks pioneer work.

Miss Cox added a personal note:

I should have liked to see a rather sharper contrast between the unrestraint of the playground and the disciplined order of the classroom.

Maybe it was in some slight acknowledgement of the justice of this criticism that Badley, in 1906, wrote a leaflet entitled 'Dancing as a school subject'!

In addition to studying the normal school subjects and participating more or less willingly in a fairly spartan way of life – cold baths, wet runs and occasional spankings from the 'Chief' – the pupils found time to mount quite regularly 'the Show', an exhibition of the arts and crafts they had produced. Then there was the starting in 'F' dormitory in 1907 of the *Bedales Chronicle*, which after brief teething troubles ran parallel to the official *Bedales Record* until the closure of the latter in 1935. Since then the *Chronicle* has continued to provide accounts of the activities of past and present Bedalians.

In 1906 the first meeting of Old Bedalians was held at the school, an annual event which was to become of the utmost significance in providing continuity and fostering loyalty to the school through the subsequent decades. In the years 1910–11 the Lupton Hall, constructed in Dutch barn style, was completed and became thereafter the cultural centre of the community – a place for merriment and worship, strenuous performance of music and drama, and quiet contemplation. Here on most nights of term there took place the ceremony of hand-shaking between pupils and staff when each individual member of the school filed past the staff and said 'Good-night'. This custom has stood the test of time in spite of occasional attempts to abolish it, especially as the size of the school increased. At this time too there was introduced the after-lunch siesta when all the pupils had to recline quietly on their beds for half an hour: only recently has this practice lapsed. 1911 also saw the return of an O.B. pupil as a member of staff, Basil Gimson. He became second master after the retirement of O.B. Powell in 1933 and he is affectionately remembered as a fine maths teacher, a wizard with timetable intricacies, a Gilbert and Sullivan enthusiast and the inspiration of madrigal singing by the 'Gimmy Quartet'.

In turning now to some evidence from witnesses of the years before 1914, it cannot be emphasized too often just how bold and unconventional – indeed, outrageous – in the eyes of some, particularly some of the Hampshire county folk, the whole Bedalian venture was. 'Enthusiastic amateurs dealing with children of cranks,' was one of the kindlier descriptions. Of the co-educational aspect there are both positive and negative reports: after the initial introduction of the three girl pupils, there would appear to have been quite strong hostility from the boys. The girls around 1904 were referred to as 'Shes'; as late as 1914–18 an O.B. boy recalls, 'we didn't talk to the Shes.' In her autobiography, Chris U. Frankenburg writes: 'Being the first girl to join my class, I was received with a shower of chalk and shouts that girls were not wanted.'*

Commenting on boy/girl relationships in those early days, one male O.B. has referred somewhat cryptically to their 'pudeur Bedalienne'. In contrast with such testimony is the careful and deliberate fostering by Badley of a certain tone, which defined the limits within which the two sexes mingled. These limits were, of course, largely determined by the very strict taboo in society as a whole on the expression by young people of overt sexual interest. Nevertheless, 'romance' of a kind undoubtedly existed; one very Old Bedalian remembers his attachment to the girl who was eventually to become his wife beginning while they were both at work in the cowshed!

The way in which self-confidence among the girls was fostered is illustrated by a reminiscence from the first Head Girl:

At the end of one term the Chief sent for me saying, 'next term I want you to be a girl prefect.' I was dazed and alarmed at the prospect, 'Must I, Chief, I don't think I can.' 'If I didn't think you could, I should not have asked you, so if I have faith in you, you must have faith in yourself.' So that was that.

More important than any of this was that from the very beginning, and however greatly modified in more recent times, the heaviest emphasis was laid on the fact that all the pupils were in the first place persons and only secondly boys and girls. As Max Plowman once remarked, 'sex is only a means of recognition, it has no end in itself, it is not an attribute of identity.'†

*Not old, Madam, but Vintage. Lavenham, Suffolk: Galaxy Press, 1975. p. 55. † Bridge into the Future. London: Dakers, 1944. p. 162.

A distinguished O.B. who was at the school between 1902 and 1911 and became well-known at the B.B.C. was Peter Eckersley. Badley wrote of him: 'I am glad to remember that the B.B.C. owes something to the hut, called by the temporary owners Wavy Lodge, where, thirty years ago, two or three of our boys carried on their voluntary experiments in what was then a new line of discovery.'

He was referring to the formation in 1908 of the Bedales Wireless Telegraphy Syndicate and in 1914 of the Bedales Wireless Society. In *The Ray* – a journal of general interest produced by members of the school (No. 3, autumn 1925), Eckersley wrote:

I have something to do with broadcasting. Broadcasting has something to do with Bedales, because each in their way represents a new point of view, and are allied, I think, in a common purpose . . . Bedales has inculcated in me at any rate the conception of liberty through service, and in the part I am allowed to play in developing these new ideas through the medium of broadcasting, I feel that Bedales helps me to foster it better.

Another distinguished O.B., who was a pupil from 1896 to 1905 and on the staff from 1911 to 1913, was Alfred Marshall, who became H. M. Inspector to the Ministry of Education from 1928 to 1948. Like several other former members of staff at a later date, he brought a dose of Bedalian freshness to the Inspectorate.

A darker and perhaps rather unexpected side to life at Bedales was the degree of bullying that went on among both boys and girls. At its worst during the first thirty years of the school's existence, though even then obviously only affecting a minority, it seems to have disappeared, though never completely, in the period between the two World Wars; perhaps it is endemic in any residential institution of children and adolescents. 'There was a lot of bullying,' writes Chris Frankenburg, 'the head of the dormitory was a very good story-teller, and the price she exacted was to spank one of the two youngest.'

E. L. Grant-Watson (1895–1904), although a reluctant admirer of Badley, was very outspoken about the shadow side of the school's early idealism. In his book* he refers to his school fellows as 'low, rough fellows of distinctly inferior types' and, somewhat extravagantly, to the regime as that of a concentration camp with tortures such as forcing small boys to swallow soap and to be sat on and trodden on in baths, making them into 'pies'. Yet he admits: 'There was a feeling of experimentation which gave zest to the teachers themselves, and if their methods were amateurish and a bit haphazard, so much the better' (p. 33).

To dip into the *Bedales Chronicle* of these years 1907–14 is to receive the impression of an intimate, active community deeply involved in congenial experiences of work and play. There were meetings of the school Fabian Society, musical evenings, lectures. A half-humorous reference was made to the growing tendency in the school to softness in daily life: 'As we all know, a great many changes have taken place at Bedales this last term, and I have come to the conclusion that the school is becoming sadly luxurious, e.g. buns for afternoon tea, glasses to drink out of instead of mugs and a fire in Mr. Garstang's classroom. It will indeed be tragic if we were to become like other people and forget we are supposed to be leading the Simple Life.' (*B.C.* 6 October 1907)

The *Bedales Chronicle* 1:9 reports on 'Bedalianism in Russia'. To say nothing of Madame Livitsky's school, the spirit of Bedales also appeared in the following places: the Forest School, the Viborg Commercial School, the Peters Commercial School, a Gymnasium in Tiflis, Caucasus, the Prince Oldenburg Gymnasium, Caucasus, and a few more. New *Letters on Bedales* by Mrs N. Jarintzoff appeared in the Russian press, and the private circles of people in Russia devoted to these principles grew. *Chronicle* 1:13 announces that 'on Saturday June 13th a small contingent from Bedales is going up to London to join the Women's Suffrage procession.'

A reminder that school work was taken seriously is to be found in the news item of *B.C.* 2:2 entitled 'Working Up for Examinations'. *Chronicle* 2:6 announces the dissolution of a semi-military institution, not readily associated with a Progressive school: 'We grieve to announce the temporary dissolution of the Corps.' Number 7 offers a definition of

---

* *But to what Purpose*. London: Cresset Press, 1946.

Bedales overheard outside its precincts: 'A place for invalids – an agricultural college – a place where they have no carpets!' Number 9, May 1909, prints an extract of a letter from George Meredith, dated 30 August 1898, after he had received the first prospectus of Bedales: 'One may anticipate for the coming generation that boys and girls associated in this manner will no longer meet as total strangers at the crisis of their lives and with the fire in their blood.'

Several numbers of the *B.C.* are devoted to a heated but serious argument between those in favour of charity to the under-privileged (the school Fee Aid Scheme planned for four children from the working class to stay in a cottage near the school) and those who opposed them on the more radical grounds that charity is a mere sop and does not tackle the problem of poverty at its economic and political roots: 'We play with social amelioration.'

Chronicle 4:1 points with justifiable pride to a review in the preceding month's *Nature* (15 September 1910) of the first publication of the Bedales School Scientific Society and contains an article on the 'Freie Schulgemeinde Wickersdorf' in Germany where, so says one of its members, 'our co-education is far more free than in Bedales'. Number 3 reports on the activities of an O.B. club in London, which among other things mounted a production in the Caxton Hall of *The Knight of the Burning Pestle*. Number 9 gives a colourful account of the whole school's outing to the Naval Review at Spithead, 'the Bedales Rose and the Union Jack flaunting gaily in the breeze.' On 24 November 1910 Ramsay MacDonald gave a lecture to the school on the House of Commons.

This chapter may draw fittingly to a close with quotations from three letters sent to Badley at the time of his one hundredth birthday by O.B.s of the pre-1914 era. The first is from a Frenchman, M. Bardot:

When I first came to Bedales, in 1908, I can remember thinking that both you and Osbos were very old men. This was probably due to the fact that you both had a beard. I am now seventy and since age is only a relative thing, I can imagine that you still looked very young at forty-three! And indeed I changed my mind very quickly when I saw you lean back in your chair and roar with laughter for the first time – it was in your study, and at me! As a new boy one had to make quite sure that one had heard correctly and that you'd said: 'Come in!' (which to my foreign ears sounded more like 'Gamine'). I had presented you with a slip and was asking for your signature on it. In my very best handwriting it read: 'Leave for Bardot to go on an exped. with P. A. Montague to photograph a jay on a bicycle.' With my poor understanding of the English language, I did not see the joke, not even when you looked at me and asked 'On a bicycle?' but you signed the slip and I was happy. The three years I was at Bedales were among the happiest years of my whole life.

The second extract is from a letter from Brigadier R. V. Rathbone (1907–13):

These were the days of Mr. Powell, Mr. Garstang, Mr. Williams ('Smirk'), Mr. Hooper, Mr. Unwin, Mr. Hodgson ('the Hod'), Miss Lamb, Miss Pearsall, Miss Simmons, Miss Thorpe, and last but not least, the Bargeant as we called the Sergeant-Major on the staff. This is not of course an exhaustive list and it does not include the greatest of them all, the Chief.

On the academic side, what I enjoyed most at Bedales was Latin and Greek in the Chief's study: when I had reached the dizzy heights of Class 1A, I remember so well, after a faulty translation, his 'Is it indeed? Look at it, look at it.' What a sense of humour he had.

There was a tremendous variety of activities and entertainment at Bedales. Out of doors, beside the ordinary games, there was riding under the Bargeant, gardening, and wide ranging whole-day expeditions a-wheel on Sundays in the Summer. Indoors there were lectures, the school orchestra, in which I played the Cello under Mr. Van de Velde, and classical music on Sundays after Prayers; debates (the Chief once told me I was always ready to oppose any motion whatsoever), photography (with an excellently equipped dark-room), the Christmas term plays (I played Henry V in 1913), boxing and Merry Evenings. The latter must, I think, have been a peculiarly Bedalian institution. Enjoyable is an under-statement – I remember in 1907 an admirable performance of *Spuffles*, a skit on *Raffles* with W. Bridges Adams (later of Stratford-on-Avon fame) in the title role, also a first rate production of *H.M.S. Pinafore*.

Once a few of us went to see the Greek play, *Oedipus Colonus*, at Cambridge. Coming home there was little time to catch the last train from Waterloo. Never had I seen any man walk as fast as the Chief did across London then. He did not actually run, but he must have walked at a good six miles an hour. We just caught the train; others of the party, thinking so furious a pace beneath their dignity, stayed the night at the town house of Lord Hugh Kennedy's father.

My time at Bedales saw the rejection by the House of Lords of the People's Budget of 1909, the death of King Edward VII, the two General Elections of 1910 and the Parliament Act of 1911. Political feeling during the first Election ran high. I belonged to the Conservative minority, and I remember that one side of the Quad was plastered with Party posters.

As to what Bedales has done for me – well, perhaps its somewhat unconventional and egalitarian outlook made me a more crusted Tory than I would otherwise have been but I have come to realise that I had an exceedingly good education there – it was of course, a privilege for anyone to be educated under the aegis of so remarkable a man as the Chief. In drafting the many orders and papers which fell to my lot during my thirty years' service in the Regular Army from which I retired in 1948, I have always tried to maintain a very high standard of English, for I love our rich and beautiful language. Perhaps I have Bedales to thank for this.

The third extract, from Norah H. Schuster, runs:

Dear Mr. Badley, if I wrote my real feelings about Bedales I think I should be accused of sentimentality. I know that you consider it all nonsense to say that schooldays are the happiest time of one's life but I can only tell you that my three years at Bedales, 1907–1910, were sheer joy from beginning to end. How could it be otherwise with such lively, kind, slightly eccentric masters – such capable, pleasant though less original mistresses, and yourself as overall guide? In those days Bedales was said by some to be deficient in scholarship, and I remember your answer to that was that you aimed at preparing our minds for learning at a later stage. Up to a point it worked, as I found when I went to college afterwards and think of the extras we had. I am still conscious of general knowledge picked up at Bedales which I should never have

B*

thought of otherwise, not to mention all the unconscious lessons from the life we led there.

It has always amazed me to hear people say that Shakespeare at school spoils him for ever, for, though I was a miserable performer of the Shakespearean heroines you thrust upon me, I have found that familiarity with those plays has increased my enjoyment of them tremendously. One of your ideas about the girls that I remember was to keep them in a minority because you considered their presence in bulk to be very dominating as compared with the boys. I was sorry when that proportion was given up, but let us hope the girls have not such powerful personalities nowadays. You also disliked the uniform green tunics which we adopted just then, as you enjoyed seeing a variety of dresses and colours. But we wanted them, and characteristically you didn't interfere over a minor issue.

I seem to be putting very trivial memories on record, but this is a letter, not a tract, and the more profound principles that moulded our lives at school are more than memories, they are a part of our very being. It is true that we did occasionally indulge in small rebellions which must have puzzled the kindly staff with whom we were on such close terms. I remember one such when I was so flattered at being taken into your confidence, that I quite forgot I had been summoned to your study for a scolding. Every day was an experience, active or contemplative warmed by goodwill. I think of Sunday evening service; Mr. Powell's music makings; Mr. Grubb's gay excursions called surveying; Miss Stalley's Language lessons with Trzebicky clowning German poetry; and Latin with you laughing heartily at Roman jokes which some of us privately thought rather crude. There was a daring joy in smiling a tolerant smile at the Deity, and I hope you will agree that it argues affection mixed with a veneration. Your last words to me when I left school were that you never wrote letters but always answered them. You have kept that promise for over forty years in handwriting that has never wavered, like my own abiding gratitude to Bedales and to you.

Before the blanket of the dark descended on Europe on 4 August 1914 there was a week-long O.B. summer meeting, described by one who attended it as 'the last happy days for a long time to come'.

ACHIEVEMENT
(1914-35)
*

CHAPTER FOUR

The Great War and the Twenties

★

In spite of wartime difficulties: catering ('Bedales' food is one banana,' quipped a young wag), heating, maintenance, decrease of boy pupils in 1916–17 and fluctuating staff membership (more than sixty changes in four years), the features of the school became steadily more clearly defined under Badley's firm leadership. In 1916 he produced a pamphlet entitled, *Notes and Suggestions for Those who join the Staff of Bedales School.** It is worth gleaning a few of his remarks from it:

Let the small mistake teach the big lesson and punishment be speedy and seldom collective.

Teaching is not telling but helping to find out.

We need not let the impartiality we aim at seem to be indifference.

The school life is to be a practical lesson in religious toleration ... Whatever be the idea that God calls up in the mind of the speaker or hearer, whether it be an idea of personality or power, of creative intelligence, of a stream or tendency, one thing is certain, it represents to us our ideal.

Martin Luther proclaimed, 'whatsoever your heart clings to and confides in, that is your God'; 'that, which concerns you ultimately is your God,' wrote Paul Tillich four hundred years later: Badley's definition for school purposes has the same ring.

Seventy per cent of pre-1914 O.B.s were combatants in the First World War, including Admiral Carpenter, an officer serving on Jellicoe's flagship at the battle of Jutland, but there

* Cambridge University Press.

were also conscientious objectors. In the year 1915–16 the school raised £500 for a French Red Cross Ambulance; Badley himself ran Current Events classes – his 'War Jaws' as they were to be remembered long after by former pupils.

In February 1914, when there were one hundred and twenty-five boys and seventy-five girls at Bedales, Badley spoke to the Heretics Society at Cambridge on the subject of co-education:

And as our leading playwright and paradox-monger says in one of his Prefaces: 'A man as intimate with his own wife as a Magistrate with his Clerk or as a Prime Minister with the Leader of the Opposition, is a man in a thousand', and there is not so much exaggeration in the paradox after all. For at marriage most people are on the footing of foreigners, with different habits of thought and life – differences of which they are conscious, the more annoyingly that they do not understand them.

Hence, the speaker implied, the argument for co-education. Although the rule for girls at Bedales was 'no corsets and hair to be parted in the middle', and although the relationships between boys and girls were heavily accented with the comradely rather than the sexual, one distinguished O.B. of that era recalls how the two sexes 'corridored' together, that is, stood leaning in somewhat romantic communication over the railings of the corridor which at first-floor level runs round the Quad. This covered-in space has always been both the crossroads and lingering point of Bedalians bent on work or play, dalliance or diversion. On one occasion the Chief remarked by way of dry if tolerant reproof, 'I hear people have been seeking double solitude in the classrooms after prayers.' Just how revolutionary the notion of a co-educational boarding school was at this period is well conveyed by the sensation created by the publication in 1917 of Clemence Dane's *Regiment of Women*. That novel describes the cloying, unhealthy atmosphere of a girl's boarding school and contrasts it with a new recently-founded co-educational school. There is a vivid description of daily life in Dene Compton, a pseudonym for Bedales: *

* London: Heinemann. pp. 218–20.

Alwynne stood shyly enough in a roofed corner of the great brick quadrangle, munching a fair imitation of a dog biscuit, and watching the boys and girls who swarmed past her as undisturbed by her presence as if she were invisible. At the boys she smiled indulgently as she would have smiled at a string of lively terriers, but of the girls she was sharply critical. They wore curious, and as she thought, hideous, serge tunics; she jibbed at their utilitarian plaits, but she conceded a good carriage to most of them and was impressed by a certain pleasant fearlessness of manner... She watched a small girl dash panting to the loggia at the opposite side of the quadrangle, where a slight man in disreputable tennis shoes leant against the shaft and observed the pleasant tumult. There was a moment's earnest consultation, and the small girl darted away again and disappeared down a corridor. The man resumed his former pose – head on one side, smiling a little; . . .

Alwynne ventured out of the corner and caught at Alicia as she passed:

'Cousin Alice! I like all his. Who's that?' She nodded towards the man in tennis shoes.

'The Head.'

'The Headmaster!'

'Why not?'

'But, but when Miss Marsh [her own Headmistress] comes in, you can hear a pin drop. Is he nice?'

'I'll introduce you.'

She did. 'Well,' said Alicia with a twinkle as they walked home together later, 'what did you think of him?'

'Cousin Alice – it was too bad of you. He just said "How do you do" and smiled politely. Then he said nothing at all for five minutes and then he clutched at one of the girls and handed me over to her with another smile – an immensely relieved one – and drifted away. I've never been so snubbed in my life.'

'You're not the first. So you didn't like him?'

'Oh! I liked him,' conceded Alwynne grudgingly.

They walked on in silence for a while.

'What's that?' Alwynne pointed to a large grey building half-way down the avenue.

'The girls' house, Hill Dene [Steephurst]. They sleep there; and have the needlework and housewifery classes, I believe.'

'Do they have everything else with the boys?'

'Practically.'

'Does it answer?'

'Why not? Girls with brothers and boys with sisters have an advantage over the solitary specimens, everybody knows. This is only extending the principle.'

Alwynne giggled suddenly.

'You know that girl he dumped me on to – she was showing me round, and we ran into some boys in the Gym. I couldn't make out why, but she jolly well sent them flying.'

'Out of hours, I expect.'

'But the coolness of it, Cousin Alice! She was a bit of a thing – the boys were half as high again!'

'But not Prefects.'

'Oh! I see,' Alwynne meditated. 'Oh! Cousin Alicia, that girl asked me to go with them next Saturday for a tramp, she and another girl and some boys. Imagine! They are going by themselves – without a master or mistress or anything!'

'Why not?'

'We don't – we crocodile. Two and two. And I trot alongside and see that they don't take arms.' . . .

'I don't think they want *ladies* here [at Dene Compton – Bedales] said Alicia. 'They are quite content if they produce gentlewomen. Your school must be peculiar.'

'Oh! No,' said Alwynne opening her eyes. 'There are dozens of schools like ours.' . . .

The great school fascinated her. It was scarce a third larger than her own in point of number, but the perfections of its proportions made it impressive. The arrangements for the children's physical well-being reflected the methods employed for their spiritual development. There was an insistence on sunlight and fresh air and space – above all space. There was no calculation of the legal minimum of cubic feet: body and mind alike were given room in which to turn, to stretch themselves, to grow.

Yes, as a foreign visitor remarked, Bedales possessed 'the advantages of intelligently used wealth', and was exploiting them wisely.

From its earliest days, Bedales paid much attention to dramatic activities, and the Chief's productions of Shakespeare's plays were memorable events for participants and audience alike – perhaps just because of their comparative lack of sophistication. In the *Bedales Chronicle* Jubilee number (1943), Barbara Burnham (1911–17) recalls these plays in an article headed 'Bedales, Acting and the B.B.C.'

Over twenty-five years ago now, a small schoolgirl of fifteen came out of the Chief's study one day in the Autumn evening after Prayers with a thin red book in her hand. As she stooped under the dimming light in the Quad to open the book and read, her heart beat fast with excitement and wonder. And, from the first moment she read those opening lines of *King John*: 'Now, say Chatillon, what would France with us?', she was living in Plantagenet England: whirled in the next scene into medieval France and nothing else existed for her. From the day she first read these lines to some days after the last school performance, she lived in those times, in those people, and moved among them more vividly than she lived outside them. Morning runs, bed-making, lacrosse, evening prep., and the rest were a dream – this play her reality. She did not learn her lines with any conscious effort – they grew into her heart and mind as if they had always been there. From the first rehearsal on that narrow, sloping, school stage, she walked as that tragic mother, filled with her anguish and tumult. And she was blissfully unconscious that her unskilled movements, her intense, amateurish voice, could belie the creation that moved so powerfully within her – and, in brief, that appearance could be so at odds with feeling. From any professional standard of acting, I know now that her performance must have been really 'lousy' (though I think the word then was 'putrid') but what she was doing, in however gauche and ignorant a manner, was the beginning of acting, and the right beginning, for acting starts with the instinct to imagine and feel another's feelings; and an urge to convey these borrowed feelings to an audience whom you will make believe what you are believing because you find in yourself some power that enables you to do so.

Reminiscing about a production of *A Midsummer Night's Dream*, the same writer comments: 'But when it came to Bottom (a character as dear to the Chief as Falstaff), back went that beard, then dark brown, pointing to the rafters;

and one evening he laughed so uproariously that he nearly fell into the narrow orchestra pit.'

Recalling her own utterly unproduced appearance in *Much Ado about Nothing*, she writes, 'Beatrice has a short soliloquy, for which I suppose I bounced down to the footlights. "This isn't Grand Opera, girl. Don't say it to us; say it to yourself." Also I remember how amused he was by a bashful Benedict: "Not on the cheek, man, on the mouth, on the mouth!" Yet in a kissing scene in *The Taming of the Shrew* his advice to the somewhat over-ardent boy and girl acting was "You needn't do it properly every time!" '

'We hurried to take our cues,' recalled one O.B., himself later to become a professional actor, 'from the girl's boot-room, so that out of a forest of black Wellingtons we would suddenly emerge into that of a cardboard Arden, or perhaps a blasted heath, or yet a street in Verona.'

It was part of Badley's educational genius to recognize the supreme importance of encouraging 'the instinct to imagine and feel another's feelings', and to provide opportunities in drama for his pupils to discover in themselves the power to do so.

In 1913 there joined the staff Mr R. E. Roper, whose influence at Bedales and elsewhere on physical education was considerable. 'Prior to his arrival Gym had consisted principally of military drill, marching, muscle developing exercises, emphasis on smartness: and woe betide the weakling or the slacker. With Roper the weakling became his special care.' (*B.C.* Jubilee Number, 1943).

P. A. Smithells, later to become Professor of Physical Education in New Zealand at Dunedin, received his inspiration from this remarkable man. Referring to war-time and the Twenties, Smithells wrote:

I do not think O.B.s realise how very far ahead of their time were our methods in health and physical education. Not only was healthy living part of the general philosophy of the Chief and those around him, but R. E. Roper was a genius and a pioneer whose influence will be felt fifty years and more hence in many corners of the world. He is the only English philosopher of Physical education with real practical knowledge . . . Roper changed physical education from Fascism to Democracy, in which the individual develops fully in the most sensitive period of his life . . . Physical Education at Bedales, thanks to the Chief's judgment in letting Roper use his methods, really did safeguard the optimum development of the individual . . . we cannot get in all schools 'little gyms', rest periods, siesta, posture checkings twice a term, monthly weighing, remedials and the occupational therapy so often used to build up confidence – but this is an aspect of education to which I and several others feel it is worth devoting our lives, thanks to Bedales.

Former members of the school began to link up with one another in adult life. In November 1917 a Bedales Club with some 220 members opened in London; two years later a debate on co-education was held there; through visits back to the school by O.B.s involved in the War the school community remained in touch with the wider world. Evidence concerning the school's internal life during this period is forthcoming from those who experienced it either as staff or as pupils. One of the former, writing to Badley in 1965, comments:

I have been living in America teaching Art and Writing and Painting ever since 1921, but I always look back to the two years when I was on your staff 1916–18, and I treasure so many memories. I was thrilled to find the whole community living up to the true spirit of the school motto – Work of Each for Weal of All – and I shall never forget the unusual educational exchange among all the teachers. It was at Bedales that I gleaned such a wealth of music appreciation. The glorious Recitals by Jessie Hall . . . the informal and delightful gatherings with Pattuffa Kennedy Fraser when she played all the Gaelic Airs from the Hebrides on her harp. Also the wonderful group singing around a peat fire at the Powells which Osbos directed with such sincere zeal. My class Prefect was Malcolm MacDonald, and I shall always remember the way he helped the school in tense times of Zeppelin raids and grim war days. (I have his ration song.) So many boys came back with the mud of the trenches on their boots, and so many we knew personally were killed. I remember the outstanding script lettering the school was noted for. It was at Bedales that I first truly realised that, generally, most creative ability is inherited. I was so lucky as to have Stephen Bone as one of the best Art students. He was amazing with both pencil and the gift of words at thirteen. Of course one remembers many things, how Roderick Hill used to excite classes of all ages when he came zooming down, looping the loop etc., right over the school and that later he became Marshal of the Royal Air Force.

A pupil (1911–16) congratulating Badley on his one hundredth birthday wrote:

We are overjoyed that you are still enjoying old age, and I doubt if any of us are really surprised at this when we remember how you strode around – apparently terribly serious but always with kindly hands and with a twinkle in your eye. Did you really buy your grey flannel 'bags' wholesale and keep them in the bottom drawer? . . . Those wonderful senior expeds. [Unaccompanied outings on foot and by cycle into the rich Hampshire countryside] in Summer on 'out' Sundays taught me to mix: we sometimes became too serious in our assessment of the values of life but I am sure that what I gained from Bedales was the ability to see and respect many points of view although your Sunday evening Jaws gave one a central set of values of one's own. Bedales must never get too stuffy. I can hardly remember one stuffy moment under your guidance, Chief. It is only later that one realises how wonderfully all-round was your upbringing of your large family, because that was what we were, happy usually, but always a family with a developed sense of loyalty to your own ideals.

In her *Memoirs of an Uneducated Lady,** Lady Allen of Hurtwood pays tribute to Badley's influence on her own life:

I was eighteen when the time came for me to leave Bedales, at the end of the Summer term 1915. I packed my trunk, said goodbye to my friends, had a good weep on the cricket pitch and visited my favourite places. I had found much happiness here and was sad to leave. My last call was to thank the Chief. To my utter astonishment he asked me to stay for another year as Head of the school. He considered, he said, that the school was becoming too lax, and he needed someone who could give the Prefects the right sort of lead. If I would undertake the task, he

* London: Thames and Hudson, 1975.

would charge my parents no fees for the year. It was like a reprieve from execution and of course I gratefully agreed. I hope I repaid the Chief's trust.

Of that there was no doubt, either at the time then or later on when this ex-Head Girl became one of the most distinguished Governors of the school.

From another girl (1915–20) comes this comment suggesting that this was the high point of Badley's reign: 'I think my time as a child was during the Chief's best.'

Further insight is provided by Sir John Rothenstein (1913–19) in a chapter in his autobiography,* entitled 'School at Bedales': 'According to the generally accepted view, any exactly defined belief was apt, by its very nature, to be discounted as an expression of narrow-mindedness; likewise everything ecclesiastical as belonging to an order which a progressive society had left behind.'

Finally, an O.B. recalls 'a cold afternoon in November 1918 at Bedales, a master stopping the game of Association Football to tell us that an Armistice had been signed.' There was a celebration bonfire on Stoner.

There are three useful points of entry into the history of Bedales in the Twenties. The first of these is the publication in 1923 of *Bedales. A Pioneer School*† 'by J. H. Badley M.A. Headmaster', dedicated 'To all those on the staff and in the School, parents and friends, to whose efforts and whose faith Bedales owes what worth it has.' This event was a signal that the school, now grown from three to two hundred and forty pupils, had emerged as a significant object on the educational landscape and was likely to remain on it. The principles and practice described in that book had already received a formal and constitutional foundation in the establishment on 5 March 1920 of the Bedales School Company and by its nomination under Article 10 of Badley as first Governor and of the Company Members (see Appendix II). The first meeting of a Board of Governors, elected by the Company, was held on 30 July 1920. In 1922 the Misses Badley, two sisters of the Chief, made over to the school the sum of £32,500 in return

* *Summer's Lease*. London: Hamish Hamilton, 1965.
† London: Methuen.

for an annuity of £1,625. During 1919–20 the War Memorial Library, designed by Ernest Gimson, was built from a fund of £10,000 specially raised for that purpose; it was formally opened in 1921. During 1923–4 the Horsley Laboratories were constructed at a cost of £5,000 left as a legacy to commemorate the two Horsley brothers, Oswald and Siward, who had both served in the First World War.

The second point of entry is a reference in one of the monthly letters Sir Michael Sadler wrote for the *Journal of Indian Education* (November 1921), which provides evidence that Bedales had been commended by a distinguished English educationist:

At this moment some valuable contributions to the art of education are being made at private schools, among them Bedales under Mr. J. H. Badley, and the Hall School at Weybridge under Miss Gilpin. Without the experiments made in the best private schools, English education would have had an impoverished tradition.

The third point of entry is through the Foreword and opening chapter of Geoffrey Crump's book, *Bedales since the War.** He himself was to bring distinction to the English teaching in the school from 1919 to 1945. It provides a valuable insight into the motives which made not only the author himself but a number of other young men and women join the staff in the period following the First World War:

When the war came to an end, most of us found it difficult to contemplate a return to our old occupations. Too much had happened to us . . . Moreover, the conviction had bitten pretty deeply into our minds, during those four revealing years, that there must be something very wrong with a social system that could bring about such an orgy of waste and misery. Those of us who had been schoolmasters must have felt this more than most. . . . The causes of the war were the direct result of the ideas that had been instilled into the youth of every European country for generations, and the war itself provided an utterly ineffective solution of the problems that these ideas created . . . I had come to realise that if I was to go back into education it must be to

* London: Chapman and Hall, 1936.

something fundamentally different. All the conventions that I had accepted and passed on without question – religious, moral, patriotic, social – I could no longer accept or pass on . . . It was clear too, that the war had not left even the Public Schools quite what they were before. But there was little hope of reforming the traditional schools from within . . . It was therefore to the 'new' schools that I turned, and fortune directed my steps to Bedales. (pp. 7–10.)

I came to Bedales a few months after the Armistice, and to one accustomed to orthodox education it seemed a strange place. It was also, to one recently liberated from the Army, a delightful place. Its most immediately striking characteristic was the atmosphere of freedom and contented activity . . . There was a holiday feeling about the whole place; everybody was healthy and happy and full of interest. It was like a big family : all on the best of terms, and all devoted to their home; it was difficult to believe that one was a member of a school staff, and a newcomer at that.*

Later in this same chapter Crump is critical of the academic standards he found in the school and of the fact that :

the boys and girls, as a whole, were contented with inferior achievement in all their activities and that there was a fairly strong and fairly universal determination to do only what they wished to do. (p. 28.)

I soon noticed even in this carefree atmosphere a certain dissatisfaction could often be detected especially among the older ones. They were beginning to feel that they were not getting anywhere.

Finally, Crump quotes the opinion of one who subsequently became headmaster of a famous Public School :

At Bedales you have begun to solve our greatest problem – that of intellectual apathy; you seem to have got everybody interested in everything, though you have done so at the expense of such things as fatigue, dissipation of energy, and a lowering of academic achievement. You have also made school life a thing which is thoroughly happy, and thoroughly healthy, another

* Author's Note : On joining the staff myself fifteen years later my impressions were precisely similar.

thing that we have not achieved. But it seems to me that in your principle of liberty you are catering for an ideal state which is not in existence, and in that sense you cannot be said to be giving children the best training for life as it now is. We gratefully recognise that your experiments are valuable, and that experiments are necessary; but we feel that your system, though based on sound ideals, is not one which is as yet suitable for general use.

That, I think, [Crump concludes], is a just criticism of Bedales as it was in the years immediately after the war. (p. 40.)

In a contribution to Badley's book* Laurin Zilliacus, himself to become headmaster of a progressive school in Finland and Chairman of the New Education Fellowship, provides further helpful insights:

Perhaps the most vivid recollection I have of the Bedales of 1908 to 1912 is of my grief — I think I may say our grief — at leaving; or to put it another way, of the depth and completeness with which the school took hold of us was for me, at least, an imperceptible process. I came with no preconceived respect for the ideals of the school; and yet in a year or two I became, as did most of my contemporaries, an almost fanatical adherent of all for which I conceived the school to stand. (p. 159.)

I returned to Bedales as a teacher in 1917. The disillusionment of this black year was settling over the world, and had me thoroughly in its grip. The first effect of returning to Bedales was that I, so to speak, lost my disillusions: the war seemed once more incongruous and a mistake, and human life full of hope and beauty . . . Yet 'it soon became apparent that not only was the standard of work low, but the standard of interest too, and all too frequently the standard of behaviour lower still.' That within three or four years these things were well on the way to reform is a tribute to the energy and self-criticism of Badley and his staff . . .

These 'new' ideas (particularly of the boys' dormitory management) were not new, they were merely a development, a form of expression in harmony with the times, of the constant purpose of the school 'to give life and to give it more abundantly.' They

* *Bedales, A Pioneer School*, Chapter 11: 'Impressions as Boy and Master'.

made authority stand more nearly for service than before, they solved (for a time at least) the acute problem of individual community and government, and they brought inspiration and happy activity where there had been doubt and discontent. (p. 175.)

Culling the pages of the *Bedales Record* and *Chronicle* for the Twenties, various items catch the eye. By a vote of two to one the school declined the offer of a German trench mortar as a relic from the War Office Treasury's Committee. In 1922, £300 was raised for the Save the Children Fund's work in the Russian famine. Carleton Washburn, Superintendent of Schools in Winnetka, U.S.A., visited the school in 1923 and commented:

Bedales, although one of the pioneers, differs in some ways most widely from the typical 'new school'. It has developed new methods of instruction and is co-educational. This latter is unusual in a boarding school, even in America. It works out admirably. One could not ask a finer, more wholesome attitude between boys and girls than one finds at Bedales. It is one of the oldest and perhaps the most progressive and alive of all of the new schools. Indeed, except for an orphanage in Czechoslovakia, Bedales was the finest school we found in all Europe.

In the mid-Twenties the School Parliament, which had been an early attempt to provide for a small measure of pupil-participation in the running of school affairs,* was turned into the School Council as a slightly larger measure of self-government; an annual Parents' (not Speech) Day was inaugurated; and O.B. meetings in the school at the end of the summer term became firmly established. Of one of these E. L. Grant-Watson, himself a distinguished but critical O.B., recorded his impressions of 'a consciousness of something which was more than a school, more than a community of present-day men and women; a consciousness of a reality in the past, present and future, which is Bedales . . . We sense a difference from the early idealism. Perhaps it is that the period of pioneering is past and that sacrifice is no longer needed or even thought about.'

In Number 38 of the *Record* (1925) it is noted that a thou-

* The Parliament first met on 12 October 1917.

sand names of past and present pupils are on the School Roll and that a Bursary Fund has been started. In February 1923 Mr G. Lowes Dickinson gave a lecture at the school on the League of Nations. A former member of the staff, Mr Wicksteed, became Headmaster of King Alfred School; another former member became Headmistress of an Elementary School in Foxton, Cambridge and wrote an article for the *B.C.* entitled 'The Beginning of Freedom in an Elementary School'. A review of Badley's *Bedales, A Pioneer School* appeared in *The Times Educational Supplement*; it stated, 'The school is one of the most remarkable and interesting educational achievements of our time.' 'Owing to the number of visitors this term,' notes the *B.C.* in July 1924, 'we are realising the necessity of training guides to conduct large parties over the school.'

O.B. Powell, second master, attended the third International Conference organized by the New Educational Fellowship at Heidelberg in August 1925 and spoke there as the Bedales delegate on 'The Release of Creative Energy in the Child'. Writing in the October and November 1925 numbers of the *Chronicle*, he reported: 'The admiration and, one might say, reverence for Bedales and its Founder repeatedly expressed throughout the Conference was positively overwhelming. In a way it made me feel that in spite of all our many visitors to Steep we have ploughed a rather lonely furrow for these thirty years.'

Occasionally, proceedings were touched by the absurd. Basil Gimson recalled one such incident:

There are some Bedalians who will smile to remember the great 'onion experiment'. We were threatened with an epidemic of influenza. The medical authorities told us that if we hung up a bag of raw onions in every room, the 'flu germs that were about to invade the human body would rush for preference to the onions (at least I think that was the idea). So we solemnly hung up our onions in every class-room, and every week a squad of onion-choppers wept at their task of preparing fresh onions, while the old germ-infested pieces were fed to the pigs. The remarkable result was that we really did keep free of 'flu the whole term. So did the pigs. I like to remember, too, that no onions were hung in the Chief's study, by order. And he remained as fit as we and the pigs.*

It is worth turning now to the witness of a varied selection of O.B. staff and pupils regarding the school in the Twenties:

I went to Bedales [writes one of them], in the autumn of 1922 at the age of fourteen and stayed until March 1926 . . . The atmosphere was strange but thoroughly friendly. I was put in charge of a kindly elder boy who showed me round and in whose dormitory (of five boys in all) I slept. The staff at that time included, besides the Chief and Mrs. Badley (Ma B.), Miss Thorpe, the boys' matron (Toips), Mr. Powell (Osbos), Mr. Gimson (Gimmy), Captain Taylor (Capt. T.) Estate Manager and Workshop master, Mr. Crump, Miss Patrick (Patters) the Housekeeper, Mr. Roper, Mr. Zilliacus (Zilly), Mr. Stuart Wilson (the distinguished musician, later Sir John Stuart Wilson) and a number of others including Miss D. R. Smith, Mr. Wolstencroft, Mr. Barker, these were all outstanding characters. My own Form Mistress was Miss Thompson, a kindly person and able teacher.

When I say things were strange, I suppose they always are for every new boy on coming to school. At that time Bedales was in the throes of the Dalton or Laboratory system. One's first problem was to understand the Time-Table. This was Gimmy's work, and the Time-Table was a marvellous piece of lines, coloured chalk and beautiful lettering. It meant little to me. But then somebody explained to me that you got from the stationery cupboard near the covered way a blank Time-Table sheet. You looked at the Notice Board and discovered (for instance) that you were in such and such a Maths set and that that set was held on certain periods in a particular room. You filled up your form accordingly, and by looking at the various lists posted on the Board eventually had your form about half-filled with periods when you attended upon a teacher. All the other periods (individual periods) were available either for work in the library or in any of the subject rooms which were vacant. This was unusual for anybody who had been to school where every period was filled with class-work and nothing was left to the pupil's discretion. I did not know when I went to Bedales that this was all experimental and in its early stages. On the whole I flourished

* 'Freedom to Experiment,' in B.C. Jubilee Number.

on the system, as I had always been a keen reader and rather a loner. My form teacher encouraged me to spend periods in the library and find my way round the shelves. At the end of that year there was a debate, and a motion was passed disapproving of the system. I was asked to be one of the speakers against the system and rather precociously agreed, but on the whole I really approved of the system. However, it did not work for everyone and later, after a large number of failures at School Certificate, of which I was one, was considerably modified. The defect was a tendency to do too much of what one liked, rather than what needed to be done. Of course, in theory, one had to show up one's work each week or month, and one's class teacher should tell one when one needed to pull up but it did not always work out like that . . . Many of us failed in French. We were then put in the charge of a marvellous French teacher, Mademoiselle Domelunksen – sister of Mrs. Kellgrin. She gave me a lifelong love of French and got us through the Exam. Many years after, she died in a fire at The Cricketers Inn where she was living in retirement.

The presence of girls was strange, but not very strange, as I came from a large mixed family. The conditions of life were fairly Spartan. The day began with Toips and her assistants taking everybody's temperature; if one had a raised temperature, off one went to the Sick Room. Then, on the rising bell, there were cold baths. The baths had been filled with cold water the night before. One stripped in dormitory and ran along the Flat [name given to that part of the main building which housed the boys' dormitories] to the bathroom and plunged in a bath and out again. The water of course overflowed, and the floor was flooded. On the Dormitory Flat each dormitory had a Dorm. Boss. If a prefect slept in the dormitory, there was also a Vice-Boss. Prefects came to bed when they liked, but the ordinary bedtime for boys was 8.50. Lights were out at 9.00, and after that talking in the dormitories was not allowed. All dormitory windows had to be wide open at all times. Evening washing was in one's own handbasin in the dormitory, but no hot water was allowed, only cold water from large, galvanised metal goose-cans. After breakfast one made one's own bed, each bed being wooden slats made in the school estate workshop. Beds were covered with 'greeneries' [green coverlets], which had to be

old Bedales in 1899.
From left to right:
Back row:
Arthur B. Girdlestone,
Malcolm C. Powell,
T. J. Garstang,
Stanley Parker,
Theodore W. Grubb
Middle row:
Lewin Cobb,
Gertrude Martin,
L. R. Schlesinger
Front row:
Gertrude Withers,
Mrs Badley, J. H. Badley,
Mrs Green, O. B. Powell

A movement class at Steephurst in 1925
Miss Hobbs is watching from the lower step.

The Chief pictured towards retirement in his familiar grey suit.

absolutely straight and smooth. The Housemaster slept on the boys' Flat, and when I arrived with my father on the first day was wearing corduroy slacks and sandals. Besides bed-making after breakfast there were 'sets'. This meant one had to go to the lavatory at a particular time. When we arrived, we were told this was very important. The 'bogs' were earth closets, and one squatted over a sort of iron frame. They were cleared every day by 'Capt. Hook' [a member of the Estate staff] with his horse and cart, who carried off the night's soil to the school sewage beds beyond the Sanatorium and laid down fresh lime and earth. Jackets were always worn and a red knitted school tie. Before mid-day dinner all, except the oldest boys and girls, lined up in the Quad for inspection by prefects. Hands had to be clean and free from ink, tie straight and hair brushed. After inspection, when the bell went, one filed into the dining hall and sat in age order.

The Chief ate at the 'top', a table which was just by the door out of his study. He usually had a boy and a girl prefect at the table as well as guests. Ma B. came occasionally. He always finished his meal with a glass of milk. He rang a small silver bell, and we were free to go. We were required to eat 'a legal minimum of meat and vegetables'.

The Quad was the great centre of life in the school. There one met friends and kept a watchful eye on the various notice boards to find out what one should do. In those days we were very modest in contact between the sexes, and the frank talk of today was unknown. In the boys' dormitories there was the usual smutty talk found amongst boys. I remember two funny incidents which were recounted in an almost hushed tone to the girls. One was when a boy fell into the bogs and the other related to the library. In those days there was a fireplace in the centre on which stood a nude Grecian plaster statue of a man. A boy climbed on the statue and by accident slipped and pulled the penis off the statue . . . In some ways we lived a very protected life. We were not allowed out of the school grounds to go to Petersfield without written leave, but in the Summer there were many Expeds. to places of interest and beauty in the neighbourhood. In 1925 the Chief's Christmas Shakespeare play was *The Comedy of Errors*. The two Antipholuses were played by Alan and Claude Scott (the Scott twins) and the two Dromios by Robin and Clement Hale (the Hale twins – grand-daughters of Ian Forbes Robertson who came to the school to give elocution lessons). Discipline was not very severe, but I think we felt sometimes we were treated too much as small children. The sweet rule is an example. Sweets were strictly forbidden. There was not much punishment; prefects' beatings were abolished the term before I came; the Chief occasionally beat a boy. Staff were addressed as Sir or Mrs. or Miss; boys were always called by their surname and the girls' surnames were preceded by Christian names or initials. I think we lacked privacy.

In recent years I have seen a good deal of schools, and I am also Chairman of the Governors of an Independent School. Much that was regarded as pioneer in our days at Bedales is now standard practice.

A former teacher of Gym and Games, a woman of twenty-four at the time, writes now aged eighty-three:

The Chief naturally comes first in my memories. His calmness – his fairness towards staff and children; Miss Hobbs, the House-mistress – a splendid woman, Mr. Roper, Gym staff extraordinary – he hated cruelty, was very outspoken and persuaded the Chief to let me use the Quad as well as the poor little Gym, previously for girls only – cricket – I was allowed to play with the boys in the odd match or two – a great honour! Cricket has been my life-long love!

Another woman member of staff from the Twenties writes:

I always tell people that nothing in my life was such an education as going to be on the staff at Bedales: also that whatever has happened to me I can honestly say that I had six supremely happy and creative years there – what more could anyone desire in life?

An old pupil of the Twenties recalls:

I was at Dunhurst [the Junior School] during its horrible modern phase. I could clean, dye, card, comb, spin and weave sheeps' wool, but could hardly read, and when taken to the Chief as an uncontrollable, rebellious child – I was ten years one month – as I looked up into his stern face I knew that at last here was a grown-up who would understand. I burst into tears and said, 'I want to do *lessons*!' The Chief continued to look stern, and then he said, 'You will come up to Bedales as the youngest child and you will sit at the back of the lowest form until you have caught up!' I came up to Bedales the next day, half-term, and enjoyed every day I was there. It gave me a confidence in life which has given me the ability to achieve all I wanted; I believe that every other child had this complete confidence in the Chief, though we all stood in awe of him. Criticism of Bedales would be that by concentrating on producing a happy and well-adjusted person they left out the teaching that the privileged owed a duty to the country and should try to get into positions of leadership. Bedalians had the best youth possible, but I don't think we paid it back.

A Professor Emeritus of the University of London and his wife taught history together at Bedales from 1919 to 1921. He writes:

When we arrived in September 1919 the school was recovering from the terrible strain of World War I, especially its spiritual shocks, and among the older children was a great questioning of values, which meant, among other things, subject teachers were constantly challenged to justify not only the views they expressed but also the utility of the subject itself. I found it very stimulating, but at the same time rather disturbing, seeing that academic standards in the school were lower than the average for Grammar schools at that time, and most of the questioning came from the more backward pupils. I think we on the staff treated our pupils with greater respect than was the case in other schools, but I felt that the Bedalians perhaps slightly overestimated the degree of intellectual and personal freedom permitted by the school. I remember our girls' team coming back after playing a match against Roedean School and being somewhat staggered to find the girls there much happier than they had expected in a school with a conventional system of discipline. Bedalians suffered from a sort of superiority complex *vis-à-vis* other schools. Critics of the school in those days asserted that it was better for a girl than for a boy.

The Chief and Osbos were, of course, the most outstanding personalities at Bedales in my time. Their single-minded devotion to their educational and social ideals was an inspiration to us all.

To me they seemed to have much in common with the people connected with the founding and early development of Letchworth Garden City, their contemporaries. I had the greatest respect and affection for the Chief and found myself, long after I left Bedales, using his scale of values as a yard-stick in my own life.

Another glimpse, this time of the Chief in action with one of his aspiring staff, gives an idea of the intimacy of communication that marked this period of the school's existence. It is taken from a letter of congratulation to him on his one hundredth birthday :

I came to Bedales with no confidence in myself as a teacher, and you gave me just that. I had always so far taught, using the old-fashioned (but then taken as axiomatic) discipline of rewards and punishments. You allowed me to experiment in teaching in the way I thought right without using any punishment for anti-social conduct but the natural result of such conduct, which involved the working out of self-government, both individual and social with my class. I enjoyed doing this, and with your help and backing, and the active interest of the staff I succeeded eventually. You believed in me and showed the children that you did. There was one awful morning I am unlikely ever to forget. We were in the Physics Lab. and I was trying to give a lesson in Physics to a class which refused to listen and indulged in a selection of miscellaneous noises calculated to annoy any teacher. I decided on written work and went out to get the paper. When I returned, I found the door of the Physics Lab. locked. As I had agreed to keep you in touch with events, I went straight to you, and you said, 'leave it to me'. I retired to the Staff Room. After half an hour or so, a small head appeared round the door of the Staff Room, and a rather tearful voice said, 'please will you come to us – we want to speak to you'. I came. I found a very sad and silent class. Some of the girls were crying. I was told – 'the Chief has been telling us what a good teacher you are'. You seemed to have spent the greater part of the time with them doing just that, but had ended up by saying that they would not be allowed to come to the school play – a punishment certainly, but I decided to take it with them, and while the rest of the school were watching the school play, my class and I sat in our classroom. They defiantly smoked brown paper made up into something that looked like cigars but smelt abominable. We got on together excellently after that, and self-government by the class worked.

In a similar letter of congratulation Rolf Gardiner, who was at the school during the year 1919–20, and who was closely allied with the German Youth Movement, wrote somewhat romantically:

The First World War was just over. The memory of two long unhappy years at Rugby School had been almost expunged by farming in Merionethshire, by the discovery of long quiet stretches of England and Wales on a bicycle, by a free-lance self-education in London attending open lectures at Colleges and Institutions, by freedom to seek and strive as one chose. Yet I was barely sixteen and still bruised by the repressions and ugliness of a Public School environment warped by war-time reversions to Victorian habits of teaching and regimentation.

My mother (perhaps with some *arrière-pensée* of her own) suggested a visit to my sister Margaret at Bedales. The Hangers above Steep were still glorified with autumn tints of red and brown, pale green and gold. The line of the Downs and Butser Hill hid the sea with their grey-blue barrier. I was entranced by a countryside of unique and captivating beauty. Within this setting of an undefiled Arcadian landscape was Bedales itself, its buildings (then without the library) homely and uninstitutional rather than of architectural merit. Yet what struck one immediately was that its grounds and parkland were totally unimprisoning: they merged and led into the surrounding countryside. The school community clustered around its home as bees in a hive. But the corollary of this was the freedom and enticement to discover and relish the flora of an abundantly varied district.

I was almost at once inveigled into joining a walk with Malcolm MacDonald and Graham Carter in the direction of Wheatham Hill. The freedom and vivacity of our talk went like wine to my head. Here was a world of exciting ideas and unconventional ideals. The naturalness and spontaneity which imbued the school seemed like some faint memory of a free existence: full of light and joy and music and expectancy. I was head over heels in love with the place and its citizens. Margaret introduced me to a passing friend, a girl of unusual beauty and character. I decided to give this girl my heart, and although I never married

c

her the basic devotion held and still holds. That evening I visited the Chief. Should my parents agree to pay the fees, might I return to school and come to Bedales for two years? I found great sympathy and understanding from one who was a stern critic of the Public School system and an Old Rugbian like myself. He gave his consent gravely and smilingly . . . I never told him about the girl. Yet perhaps in his intuitive way he already knew somehow. But I had fallen in love with Bedales as well, and that was basic too.

One more pupil's voice from the Twenties strikes an authentic and delightful note:

My memories of life at Bedales are innumerable: adolescence is in any case an intense time of life. I never think it is fair to give a school the lion's share of either blame or praise for the people it turns out: so much has been determined in them already. I came from a family non-conformist in temperament. For such children Bedales was a haven, where they were allowed to grow and not be crushed by the pressures of conformist society; where they had a good chance of becoming pioneers or creators rather than merely misfits. Of my teachers I think particularly of Geoffrey Crump and Innes Meo, whose enthusiasms were communicated to me. I lacked self-confidence, and gained some through success in sports, getting good parts in your Shakespeare productions and being Head Girl. Then there was the magical social side: Summer expeditions on the Downs, and your Camp in North Wales and at Buttermere. We were a community, still small enough for individuals to thrive in.*

A word is in place here about the Chief's camps. The following comes from an account of them by Richard Henry, writing in the memorial volume, *John Haden Badley*, produced in 1967:

About the time that Bedales moved to Steep, Mr. Badley started to invite a few boys to camp with him in the Summer holidays, and in 1905 girls were also invited. So began an annual event dear to the Chief's own heart both as an additional feature of the full life he wanted Bedalians to embrace and enjoy, and as a holiday which he himself found most satisfying. It must, for

---

* There were not more than two hundred, including staff and pupils in the main school.

many O.B.s, rank among the happiest memories of Bedalian life. Memorable not only as a pleasant rewarding holiday, or a first introduction to camping, hill walking, climbing and so on, and as extended O.B. meetings for catching up on old friendships, but perhaps most of all for the privilege of being with the Chief at leisure, seeing his relaxed joy on working on those excellent water colour sketches, his intense pleasure in the games of chess played lying in the sun, and walking with him over the fells and hills.

Over the years sites were selected all over the country, from Devon to Derbyshire, Eskdale to Exmoor, Sannox to St. Ives; as distant as Glen Brittle in Skye, as close to home as the San Field. But the Lake District was always the Chief's own favourite area and perhaps most popular with Bedalians – indeed the *Chronicle* records in 1922, 'Kinnell has emigrated to New Zealand, no doubt in protest against camp being moved from the Lakes!'

It is not surprising that campers attended regularly year after year, and frequently one person became Chef and Organiser for several years. Rodney Straker, for instance, in the years preceding the last war, Lupton before the 1914–18 war, and in 1925 we find Kathleen Wilson recorded as 'acknowledged Stewmaster and Grandmother of all camps'. But the washing-up ritual remained throughout; all stood round, tea-towels at the ready, waiting for the Chief to rinse each article and throw it to someone to dry. Woe to anyone whose attention wandered; with uncanny accuracy a cup still half-full with hot water would hit one fair and square.

Certain other features repeated themselves – a bathing pool, if not naturally available, was soon constructed. In Eskdale in 1913 two were made, one 3-feet deep and another 5-feet deep, becoming known as the Inferior and Superior Wallows. I recall another two-bath site, twenty years later at Ogwen in North Wales. Served with running water by diverting a small stream, these were known as the Upper and Lower Baths (temperature did not encourage wallowing).

The Chief continued to hold his camps after his retirement to Cholesbury and found tremendous pleasure in retaining this share of Bedalian life. His successor [Mr Meier] of course was equally keen, he loved camp life and was a prodigious walker. What better or more congenial atmosphere for long discussions together (and for many hard fought battles over the chessboard)? When Meier successfully re-started the camps in 1949 at a new site at the foot of the Cnycht in Wales, it was hardly surprising that many O.B.s of a wide age range were anxious to come, and it was wonderful to have the Chief himself once more among us. Everyone will have their own most vivid recollection of camps – perhaps sunrise seen from Harrisons Stickle, or Fortingall in 1914 when the local Bobby puffed up to the site so many times to decide whether one O.B. was an Austrian spy, or of those wet days spent in tents playing endless games of pontoon for astronomical stakes (in dry beans), or of Meier positively galloping up and down Goat Fell. But almost certainly one of the most pleasant memories is of the Chief in the boys' tent in the evening, pillows and hurricane lamps arranged just so, reading aloud in that splendid voice to the assembly of tired, content, blanket-huddled campers as they sipped cocoa from dented, aluminium bowls.

Bedales, which had been on the Board of Education's List of Efficient Schools since 1 August 1911 and had been last fully inspected in November 1911, received a full Inspection from the 25 to 27 May 1927. Three extracts from the report make a fitting close to this chapter :

1. The position of the present Head is one of absolute authority. He is specifically mentioned as the first Governor of the Company and the first Chairman of the Governors.
2. The school differs from the usual type of school, and stands for educational methods peculiar to itself, so that if a Master doesn't fit into the school, and is out of sympathy with its ruling idea, it is impossible for him to work at his best there.
3. Bedales is an interesting school, with, as far as the Inspectors could judge in such a short time, a strong life of its own. Its establishment and continuance has been a striking example of courage and enterprise and stout honesty of purpose. Its main purpose clearly is to make its pupils self-reliant and mutually helpful. This it achieves.

CHAPTER FIVE

Towards the Founder's Retirement

★

During the period 1927–35, which marked the culmination of Badley's Bedales, the school necessarily developed a new stance towards the outside world. This came about partly on financial grounds, for, lacking any kind of endowment fund, Bedales felt the effects of the economic crisis of 1929. Pupil numbers in November 1932 were lower than at any time since 1908. This made the Governors determined to rectify the long-standing weakness of living off borrowed money by launching an appeal in 1934 for £30,000. This new attitude was in particular brought about by the announcement by Badley in November 1933 of his forthcoming retirement and the tremendous problem this created for the Governors in finding and appointing a successor. A special meeting at 10 Downing Street was arranged in May 1934 by Malcolm MacDonald (O.B.) at the invitation of his father the Prime Minister, Ramsay MacDonald, who had sent two of his sons to Bedales. Its effect was to make the school and its work known to a wider circle than those who already had personal connections with it.

At this stage, it is worth making the point that school life at Bedales proceeded on a normal basis, marked by regular lessons at which attendance was compulsory, by the usual games of football and cricket, and by a discipline which was firm and effective without being oppressive. Features which differentiated Bedales from many other schools were the small classes, individual pupil attention, special emphasis on the arts and very friendly relations between staff and pupils – this last being one of the few constants in the entire history of the school.

One former member of staff, who later became a County Director of Education, places his finger on the factor of trust: 'There was an inbuilt framework of custom and practice to support this trust. It would not be an exaggeration to describe this as the genius of the school.'

Another, who later became headmistress of a girls' Grammar School, writes:

At one time there were four old members of Cheltenham Ladies College on the staff, and I had the feeling that there was something in common between the liberal view of education of the 'reluctant pioneers' of girls' education [the title given to a book for the centenary of the Headmistresses' Association] and the Bedales outlook, and such 19th Century pioneers as Thring of Uppingham and Sanderson of Oundle – which was perhaps why we felt at home. Such people felt that education was concerned with all sides of human activity and development, not with a limited selection of subjects, that all-round development was what mattered, and that fun and friendship were a part of this. I sometimes wonder whether this wide view of education is only possible to men in whom the underlying feminine principle has been developed. The untempered masculine principle seems to me more concerned with power than with people. I think the effect of Bedales and other such schools has been felt in the widening of the curriculum in all schools – the far greater attention paid to music and art and drama and varied voluntary activities. This effect was achieved, I think, by the freedom the Chief gave to the series of staff who streamed through the school to experiment with methods and subjects and to learn far more than they could in a more rigid environment. I have never forgotten the support the Chief gave me: 'What do you advise?' he asked on some subject about which I knew nothing but had quickly to get to know! I found co-educated boys extremely pleasant to deal with: they could treat a woman as a friend and colleague and a woman at the same time. I was not sure that Bedales was always the best place for the flibbertigibbet type of girl.

Although there was no doctrinal religious teaching at Bedales, I think that the whole atmosphere was more sympathetic to spiritual values than is that of some of the modern State Comprehensives which are so determined *not* to give religious teaching or where such teaching is given reluctantly and inadequately by people neither equipped to give it nor desirous of so doing. What was given at Bedales was genuine and first-hand and valued as such.

Hu and Lois Child, who joined the staff in the 1930s and later became joint heads of Dartington Hall School, recall the figure of Badley as they saw him then:

A tall, spare, bearded figure, very much a man of habit, never varying his dress or his daily routine. His material demands were small, and there was a simplicity of life at Bedales which was one of its most endearing qualities . . . He was in some ways a curiously remote man, but though remote there was no doubt at all that it was very much his school to which one came. It was as though his faith in co-education, in non-competitiveness and in creative activity had gained such reinforcement from the new ideas of the thirties that this old school was able to give young people like ourselves an entirely new outlook.

Kenneth Barnes, another member of staff, who later started a school of his own (Wennington Hall), comments on 'the feeling of wholesomeness and life that Bedales gave me in comparison with any previous school experiences'. It was he who introduced the study of Social Biology, complementing the teaching of the anatomical aspects of sex relationships with, amongst other things, the personal and emotional aspect.

Finally, an O.B., who was on the staff for many years writes:

It is probable that what we learnt from participating in a way of life was at least equal in importance to what we learnt in the classrooms. Gradually, perhaps mostly unconsciously, we absorbed something of the enthusiasms and attitude to life of the Chief and his assistants. Sincerity and kindness were held to be of greater importance than the conventions of social prestige and class distinction. We were encouraged to think for ourselves and to form our own judgements. The basic assumption that each of us was to some extent responsible for the welfare of the community was sometimes effectively underlined by a stern 'Does that help?' from the Chief when some irresponsible or thoughtless misdemeanour had been committed.

This is perhaps a good place to comment that there were always two levels of social life at Bedales, the staff's and the pupils'. Although, on the whole, each remained strangely ignorant of the affairs of the other, there were inevitably occasions when the lives of both could become complicated by strong emotional attachments – but also enriched. Where adults and adolescents live side by side in the same community, this is neither to be wondered at nor regretted, provided that they trust each other. To a high degree – which runs counter to the findings of Jonathan Gathorne-Hardy* – this condition has prevailed at Bedales and accounts largely for the delightful flavour of the relationship between them.

Asked for his recollections of Bedales at the end of the Twenties and beginning of the Thirties, one O.B. picked out three salient features of the school: its approach to religion consisting in a deep belief that God is Spirit and God is Love; its emphasis on the importance of the individual; and its emphasis on telling the truth and assuming that others also tell the truth. Accompanying these was the constant provision of opportunities to examine things in depth and to ask questions. He concludes:

I was very happy at Bedales, but I sometimes question the education which I had. For example, I was not stretched and set targets difficult to attain unless I set them myself. Also I think we Bedalians tended to consider ourselves rather special people, and of course we were not. The emphasis on telling the truth created a Utopian element in our lives at an impressionable age, and I have found it difficult to really realise that the world is not like that.

An O.B. girl of this period recalls how:

One November in the early Thirties, the Chief was standing at the edge of the Quad, near his study, as he so often did, leaving himself available for approach. I asked him how things were. He said he was very unhappy. He explained that fireworks had become too lavish and were providing too much disparity of ostentatious wealth among the pupils, and so they had been

* *The Public School Phenomenon*. London: Hodder and Stoughton, 1977. Chapters 15 and 16.

banned for that year. One boy got up and in the dark and rain had let his off on the top pitch, all by himself. As he returned (before 6.00 a.m. I think) blackened and wet, he was caught by a master and, said the Chief, 'The miserable man has sent him to me. He shouldn't have seen him.'

The extracts which follow below from the letters of O.B.s help to portray the quality of school life:

I was at the school from the autumn of 1927 (youngest child in the school) to the end of the Christmas term of 1933 when my parents precipitously removed me because they didn't like the sort of person I had become through the influence of the school.

Since my knowledge of the school is so very out-of-date (I have only been back twice I think, although I really love the place) I can only compare my knowledge with the schools I came to know through my children. In my recollection it seems to have been the most child-orientated place that I have ever known. The Chief certainly had Greek ideas about the whole man, but I think this was overlaid with the work of each for weal of all, which genuinely in my opinion gave to the individual child a sense that what it did was valued, even if the child was not main-stream. This it seems to me was coupled with very high standards, so that the atmosphere of the institution was not sloppy. I suspect that the standards were as high as in any of the better Public Schools or Grammar Schools in the academic field. I had no sense while at school that I worked hard at academic subjects, indeed I am not at all broadly educated, but I managed to get into Cambridge without any difficulty despite having been ill for a year after being taken away from Bedales.

Looking back I think the nature of the co-education was puritanical and unpermissive, but the illusion of sexual freedom was most cleverly fostered. I also think that it must have led many an unsuspecting female into terrible scrapes in later years, having inculcated the idea that it was possible to have genuine friendships with people of the opposite sex, without there being any sexual content in them. This may have been particular to me, but I think it was a genuine manipulative process.

The youth of the staff (in general) and the free and easy atmosphere with the staff, so that as one grew older, the intellectual

c*

range and discussion possible were extremely stimulating, proved to be an excellent preparation both for University and for life. There really was time for talk and for leisure. I suspect that perhaps the library, except as architecture, was not quite so first rate as we were led to believe, but it did teach the young to use a library and how to search for information and learning.

For me the countryside and the freedom to walk and to explore were the most important single things in my time at Bedales: nothing I am sure arouses the emotion of adolescents more than beautiful scenery, and the freedom to be in it, to lie on it, to smell it. It still influences my reaction to all landscape, I mean the open Downs and the Hangers.

The following is an illuminating extract from a letter to Badley on his one hundredth birthday:

Of my time spent at Bedales, from 1923-36, I have many memories, but the three most vivid are connected with yourself. I shall never forget the happiness I felt when you cast me as Puck in *A Midsummer Night's Dream*, your last Shakespearean production at Bedales. I had determined to be an actor, when I was three years old, and had never wavered. You gave me my first opportunity.

One day with a razor pencil-sharpener in my hand I was scrapping with a boy and made a nasty cut on his leg, which necessitated a couple of stitches. I was profoundly shocked, by what I had done, never having even been conscious of having something in my hand that could cause such an injury. By the time I saw you, I was feeling like a psychopathic thug, having been admonished by staff and fellow pupils alike. I remember saying to you, 'I never wanted to injure anyone, but nobody believes me!' You looked at me, then said, 'I do.' I think it was at that moment, although probably unaware of it then, that I realised that those in authority could be one's friends, and that teachers and pupils need not be in opposition to one another. Looking back on it, objectively, I realise that had I been dealt with by someone less human, and less skilled in understanding the young, than yourself, I might well have ended up in a Juvenile Court. To me that was your genius. You never talked down to any child, you never dismissed their opinion nor their point of view.

During 1931–2 the New Education Fellowship held a big conference in Nice – eighteen hundred educationists from fifty-two countries – at which Bedales was represented. Possibly this was the high-water mark of the original progressive school movement, and it may be significant that it occurred in the aftermath of world economic crisis and on the eve of the rise to power of the European dictators. That the school was not entirely isolated from either of these phenomena is shown by the concern felt by at least some sections of staff and pupils for the unemployed in Britain and demonstrated by the organization locally of work camps for the unemployed to which Bedalians contributed their voluntary services. The other proof of this is the generous way in which the school admitted the children of refugees from Nazi Germany, which injected a novel academic vigour and sexual maturity into the community.

It is, however, over the close of the Chief's reign that we shall now linger, for although there were to be further occasions for commemorating his achievement, such as the Jubilee celebrations of 1943 and 1953 and his own one hundredth birthday in 1965, it is essential at this point to bring the protagonist of the story into the sharpest possible focus as he takes his professional curtain call. It was a moving occasion when, aged seventy, he gave his farewell Jaw, ending with the words of Socrates, 'I go to die, and you to live, but which of us goes to the better thing, is known only to God.' The fact that he then lived on in retirement to the age of 102, far from detracting from the significance of this occasion, merely provides still further evidence of his immense vitality. Three testimonies to the man from O.B. pupils and a letter to *The Times* signed by a list of his distinguished admirers, make a fitting conclusion to this part of the history of Bedales. A prelude to these are some lines from Osbos entitled:

'The spirit of Record bids the Founder Farewell'

The pen (J-nibbed) I see you now lay down,
(on fountain pens you ever seemed to frown)
Shift in old Parker's chair towards the fire
And, with a shrug, consign the job to Meier.

The first extract is taken from a letter to Badley written in 1965 by O.B. Barbara Burnham, who had become eminent in the field of broadcasting and drama:

Dear Chief, 'A Hundred Years Old' – I remember a Spanish play with that title that I once produced and played in at an O.B. meeting; in which the Centenarian was both the wisest and the youngest member of his large family. And that is how I and I am sure many many Old Bedalians think of you now. We think of you as both the wisest and the youngest of your very large family. Because, Chief, you always taught us to say 'Yes' to life, never 'No'. You taught us not only how to live best in the present, but how we could and we should live best in the future – whatever changes might come.

The second extract runs:

I first knew the Chief, insofar as a small boy can be said to know his Headmaster, in 1910. In point of fact the tall, bearded and rather severe-looking figure, passing across the Quad or along the corridors with long silent strides, and looking neither to right nor to left, inspired feelings of awe which lasted most of my school life.

His public image indeed could be formidable especially when angry, when, with a brow like a thunder cloud, and a few quiet but well chosen words he would reduce his audience to pulp . . . Though neat and tidy he made no concessions to his tailor and I never remember seeing him in school in anything but his easy fitting double-breasted grey flannel jacket and the black plimsolls with a little hole in the top to accommodate his bunion. But, with his noble head and his innate dignity and unselfconsciousness, few of his visitors, however exalted, can have given much thought to his clothes.

When you got past his outward image, however, you quickly found an impish sense of humour and a warm humanity. Nothing delighted the Chief more than clever nonsense or a good anecdote. He would throw back his head and roar with laughter, piling one piece of logical absurdity on another . . . He trusted people. Nothing was ever said of course. It was just that this was implicit in his whole relationship with those around him. They responded without knowing and without asking what made them do so and very few ever let him down. When he shook hands and said goodnight after Evening Service, looking into your eyes with that grave but kindly gaze, you felt that he was your friend. And so he was, of course. Too much trust like too strong loyalties, is not of course necessarily compatible with realistic assessment of human beings, and a common criticism of the Chief related to his choice and retention of some of his staff. In this as in finance and business matters, he could be extremely unworldly.

The third extract consists of Basil Gimson's farewell to Badley at the O.B. meeting of 3 August 1935:

There was once an official of the town of Titipu called Pooh-Bah who combined in his person many offices. Though I lack something of that official's rotundity, I can claim to speak now as an Old Boy, as a member of the staff, and as parent; and in these capacities I should like to recall some scenes during the past thirty-nine years with the Chief. First some scenes which will be familiar to nearly all of us. The Latin classes, sitting uneasily under that severe glance, that sometimes softened into a kindly smile when we'd made a particularly happy guess. We were not quite sure whether we liked Latin, but how we looked forward to the evening classes in Roman History. Just as a child loves the stories told at bedtime by his father so we eagerly listened to these stories of far-off days told by a master teller.

Other scenes will perhaps be not so familiar. How many know that the Chief was the first Art master? Drawing and Painting we learned with him or tried to, and I can remember my astonishment as a small boy at being told that it was not at all incorrect to place green and blue close together in the same design. I wonder how many here have taken shorthand with the Chief? I still have in my possession a postcard written in that remarkable hieroglyphic which is nearly as difficult to read as the Chief's own minute handwriting. Then the games of football, when at half-back one came into collision with a hard body on the out-side-wing and wished that there was a more ample covering on that spare frame. Then the rare occasion when glancing out of a classroom window in the early morning we caught sight of a figure striding off to catch a train for London in top hat and, was it, sand shoes? Whether on that journey he was bound for the dentist or the Derby, history does not relate. And in the holidays more than once it has been my privilege to be in a small party of Bedalians, guests of the Chief, at the Shakespeare Festival at Stratford. And can you imagine the joy to us youngsters at being taken to the theatre every evening for a whole week? The Chief certainly has understood how to make the best use of his holidays and to this must be ascribed his wonderful youthfulness. When holidays had arrived he was able to throw aside completely the cares of the term. I am reminded of the following incident which happened in the very early days of the school. A French boy was returning to his home in Paris, but after two days, had not yet arrived; so an anxious telegram was despatched by the parents: 'Where is my Pierre?' Back came the reply: 'Don't know', and the Chief went off for his holidays. So our knowledge of the Chief has been built up from a thousand of such scenes of laughter, respect and admiration not untinged with awe. In these happy days of school we came gradually to understand that he was teaching us a way of life. We left with an abiding sense of the rightness of right and the folly of wrong and we came to realise that true happiness of life is to be found not in the pleasures of the moment but in seeking the things of enduring value.

On 27 October 1934, under the heading, 'A Pioneer of Education', the following letter appeared in *The Times*:

Sir, the retirement is announced of a pioneer of modern education whose work has been of greater importance than is commonly realised.

In 1892 [sic] Mr. J. H. Badley founded Bedales School, the first co-educational boarding school, as a protest against the formalism and narrowness of the Public School of his day. Although he was a rebel he was an idealist; he believed in evolution, not revolution. Today he has lived to see much that he advocated in the teeth of considerable opposition beginning to be accepted as the principles of modern education. Among the most important of these are the better understanding between the sexes, the fostering of social and international goodwill, a new vision of work by which the many activities of mind and body may be pleasurably employed for their own sake, not in fear of punishment or hope of reward; realisation of the importance of the arts in education and the greatest possible measure of liberty of thought and action that can be achieved in an ordered community. Mr. Badley is a man of retiring, almost ascetic, habit, and the public is as yet hardly aware of the great task to which he has devoted his fortune and life-work. It is for these reasons that we are anxious that the present opportunity should not be lost, on the occasion of his retirement, to pay a tribute to him as one of the great educationists of his generation, and as a man of vision, selflessness and inspiring singleness of aim.

Yours faithfully, [signed] Allen of Hurtwood, Norman Angel, Lilian Bayliss, Muirhead Bone, Horder, Julian S. Huxley, Oliver Lodge, J. Ramsay MacDonald, Cyril Norwood, Percy Nunn, Michael E. Sadler, A. C. Seward, J. P. Strachey, R. H. Tawney, John J. Withers.

ADAPTATION
(Since 1935)

★

CHAPTER SIX

Bedales under the Succession

★

Since the retirement of its Founder there have been four headmasters of Bedales, F. A. Meier (1935–46), H. B. Jacks (1946–62), T. W. Slack (1962–74) and, since 1974, C. Patrick Nobes. During the period of their headmasterships the school has in considerable measure adapted itself to the pressures of society outside in such matters, for example, as fees, academic expectations and a more permissive morality. At the same time it has preserved, indeed guarded jealously, a number of its traditional features such as mixed-age groups in dormitories, fostering of the aesthetic impulse, close and friendly relationships between staff and pupils, and a strongly questioning attitude to life in general. In the words of a former member of the staff:

Bedales has changed continuously. It is a marvellous example of the evolving school. There have been no revolutionary changes, no great dramas. Things have unfolded, the implicit has become the explicit . . . it was an educational laboratory, and I among so many others was able and free to try out educational ideas in curricula content and in method and became much wiser (educationally at any rate) as a result.

What follows now is an attempt to capture the elusive spirit of the adaptative process through four phases, lasting from 1935 until the day before yesterday, without losing sight of the personal contributions made by each of the four successive headmasters and their staff to Badley's legacy. I am fortunate in being able to draw on a document, prepared for domestic publication within Bedalian circles.*

* *Bedales 1935–1965. Memories and Reflections.* 1978.

I. SURVIVAL

The appointment of F. A. Meier was made by the Board of Governors in the knowledge that the future of the school depended on three things: first, the need for re-assurance domestically and publicly that the Bedalian tradition would in essentials be preserved; secondly, the placing of the school on a professionally sound financial basis after years of benevolent but amateurishly administered charity; thirdly, the necessity of raising the overall academic levels of study. A few eyebrows were raised at the manner of Meier's appointment – through private recommendation – and at the fact that he had no previous experience of running a boarding school, let alone a co-educational one, and that he had not himself been associated with the progressive school movement. Aged 48, he had previously been on the staff of Rugby School as senior science master and housemaster, and had built up for himself a brilliant reputation as a teacher. His ten years of office wiped away any doubts, because of his teaching skill but even more because of his personal gifts of vigour and integrity, which made their mark on the school. Not only did he do what it was hoped he would do, but, like a squirrel, he also hoarded the precious resources of the school's assets in such a way as to ensure its survival.

One O.B. who was a boy in the school at this time of transition, has commented: 'So Bedales welcomed its new Headmaster, and gradually the school changed, for Bedales contrived to be what it had always been: a progressive school.' That this was so was owed largely to Meier's successful vanquishing of a not unnatural prejudice expressed in such a remark as, 'The Chief wouldn't have done it that way.' He refused to allow the community to look backward with nostalgia to a golden past. Official recognition of this achievement is to be found in the Board of Education Inspectors' Report of June 1938:

In general, on the material side as indeed on the administrative, intellectual and social side, the school has shown that, under the wise guidance which it has enjoyed, a difficult period has been successfully passed. (p. 2.)

Under its Founder the school passed successfully through the pioneer stage of many-sided development. Today stability and permanence have been achieved but fortunately without any symptom of stagnation or complacency. (p. 21.)

With the departure of Badley, the unified command by one man of the whole school had necessarily to undergo modification. This took two forms: first, an increase in influence and responsibility for the housemistress, not only over at Steephurst but in the general life of the school; secondly, a redefinition of the relationship between the housemaster on the boys' Flat, and the headmaster occupying an adjacent portion of the same main building. This was known as the 'Wing' and, during the first four headmasterships, entertainment at weekends and in the evenings for small groups of pupils was provided here consecutively by Mrs Badley, Mrs Meier, Mrs Jacks and Mrs Slack. A similar practice has been continued in the new residence built on the estate for the headmaster in 1973. The role of second master continued to be vitally important but essentially supportive. It is fair to comment that from this time onwards there always tended to be a tension, now slight and now acute, between the house staff on one side and the academic staff on the other, regarding their respective functions. Another small, but not insignificant, way in which the school changed during the late Thirties was through the introduction of the use of christian names between pupils and most of the staff. This increased bond of informality led to improved relationships and no loss of respect where respect was due.

Although at the end of his first three years, Meier could be congratulated on having improved the school's financial position and academic reputation and also on having established himself firmly in the saddle, his sternest test was still to come with the outbreak of the Second World War in September 1939. The school opened up immediately after the declaration of war in case it were needed to receive its own pupils or other evacuees from London, but in fact only a few of the former turned up before the normal date of opening of the autumn term. Inevitably there was some sense of strain and uncertainty: trenches dug hastily near the upper football field, gas mask parades, the departure of some staff for active service, the busying of others with local defence and air-raid precaution activities and then the honest dilemmas of conscientious objectors. There was also the question whether the school itself would be permitted to continue on its present site, while to these concerns must be added the fact that by the summer of 1940 a third of the pupils had been withdrawn. However, as Mrs Meier, the indomitable partner of her husband in all his work, remarked, 'during those very months the school recovered the spirit of community of the early years,' and by July 1941 numbers were picking up again. A threat from the authorities to take over Bedales and turn it into a war-time hospital was successfully averted and despite air-raid warnings, though they were a nuisance, there was no bomb in the neighbourhood until the flying bombs came towards the end of the war. 'Did you see Freddie timing a Doodle-Bug over Butser?' one small boy was overheard saying, 'Who could be nervous after that?' commented Miss Hobbs, the Housemistress. Nevertheless, an extract from the *B.C.* of 6 July 1940, serves as a reminder of the strain under which the school community was living:

Our reserves of sleep and resources in organisation have been severely taxed during the last few weeks. Numerous alarms, luckily from our point of view fairly peaceful ones, have necessitated drastic cuts and alterations in the Time-Table . . . early bed and late breakfast. Still, they have taught us the good and bad points of our A.R.P. system, and some of the luckier ones have acquired the sensible (but elusive) art of sleeping in the trenches. Every single person on the Estate has now been provided with a tin hat. Volunteers over sixteen have been manning an Observation Post under the command of the Steep L.D.V. [Local Defence Volunteers] and have consequently been heard prowling about at the most unlikely hours of the night. A few of the girls have been helping to serve refreshments to evacuees at Collyers Maternity Home.

Some Bedalians were in the Petersfield Air Training Corps from the start. It was difficult to strike the correct balance between encouraging the pupils to respond to calls for the war effort and keeping them to their proper task of lessons.

Meier often gave sage counsel to his colleagues on this matter. An example of the concern felt by the boys and girls for what was going on outside their safe little community was the creation of HEFOLO (Help for London). 'For some time,' reported the *B.C.* of March 1942, 'the school has been sending help to the Borough of Shoreditch in the form of presents and pictures for air-raid shelters: in the same term flowers were sent to London by carter once a week.' Some parents expressed anxiety about the strength of left-wing views being expressed by a few staff and older pupils during the early months of the war. Meier took a definite line with regard to this; he favoured complete freedom of speech but reminded his colleagues how important it was for staff to distinguish between free expression of opinion and the one-sided unloading of belief by adults on children not equipped emotionally and intellectually to retaliate.

Dr L. R. Wood, the geography master, who later became headmaster successively of Beccles School and Brockenhurst County School, has contributed the following account of what happened to the Bedales farm in war-time:

When the war broke out, Whiteside was Farm Manager, and I was asked to become Chairman of the Food Production Committee – the aim being to make the school as far as possible self-sufficing in food supply. When he left, I was asked to take charge of the farm until a replacement was found and I continued in charge until July 1943 when we moved to Beccles. So I was left with the task of ploughing up a run-down dairy farm. My qualifications were limited. I guaranteed to supply the kitchen with at least forty gallons of milk a day – rising to seventy gallons or more during May – and to ensure that we had enough potatoes to last the school throughout the whole year. Higgins the gardener, on his side, was to see that we should not have to buy vegetables and as far as possible be self-sufficing in fruit. Meat, of course, was rationed but I managed to secure a licence to kill two pigs a term outside the ration as they were largely swill-fed. Any popularity I enjoyed during the war was mainly due to roast pork. It was delicious. We already had a large flock of hens, and eggs were now stored during the holidays, if necessary in water-glass, rather than being sold in Petersfield market. For the first time the farm began showing a profit. It rose eventually to over £400 p.a. As the war continued I used outdoor work squads [*see* p. 108] to cultivate odd patches unsuitable for farm machinery and to pick produce for sale – usually catch-crops such as white turnips or the tender shoots of thousand-headed kale.

We were surrounded by R.A.F. and army camps, and green stuff of all kinds met with a ready sale at high prices. I arranged with the Staff Common Room Committee that half the value of all crops picked by outdoor work squads should be credited to the Committee and used to buy furniture or other amenities for the Common Room. I believe that one winter the Common Room shared £45 with the farm. Early in the war Dr Carr, a neighbour Governor, had given us the use of his two fields, so the total area of the farm was now about one hundred and ten acres. He was delighted when one year Bedales Farm headed the winter milk averages for our district, No. 5 District.

By the time of the V-Day Picnic in the summer of 1946, it had become clear just how well Bedales had weathered the storm under its eccentric headmaster, a man in appearance like the comedian Will Hay, but so resolute and determined in performance: 'He dithers and dithers and dithers,' the Chief was once heard to remark, 'and then he does the right thing.' In the words of one member of staff he 'had the stupendous task of keeping Bedales on the same high plane set by the Chief. He set a good example to the whole school by his devotion and splendid vigour. And perhaps very few people realise what a strain he must have been under during all the war years. The responsibility was enormous.'

At the O.B. meeting of 1946, when Meier knew he was shortly to retire, he paid the following tribute to Irene Hobbs, the housemistress who had worked so closely with him; it is worth quoting not only in her honour but also as an indication of Meier's own genuine modesty and sensitivity: 'I am proud to be able to make this confession before you tonight that I have learnt more from Miss Hobbs about education during the last eleven years than from any man or any other woman alive.'

She said of him, 'It was, I think, this quickness to sense the fundamentals which Bedales tried to stand for, even though how to achieve them might seem a tangle, together with his faith in individuals, which first bridged for us the difficult gap after the Chief's retirement. How his endearing mannerisms stimulated the school!'

Paying his own tribute to Meier, Badley wrote: 'Writing about Mr. Meier is like trying to fix a piece of quicksilver on paper.' To the man who was to succeed him, Meier remarked: 'You won't find it easy, but at least you won't be succeeding a Founder.'

At Christmas 1946 the school put on a dramatic entertainment called *Cavalcade* as a way of saying farewell to Meier: it was a spontaneous expression of the love he had won from the whole community.

Writing in *The Times* of 23 February 1954, when Meier died unexpectedly early after another short but distinguished career as Senior Lecturer in Science at the London University Institute of Education, Michael Thomas wrote:

Only an alert, enthusiastic and essentially practical mind could have ensured the steady and permanent transition from experiment to establishment. Meier achieved this without once encroaching on the freedom and flexibility of the school's methods and at the same time without diminishing the pupils' sense of security at a time when the war was disrupting education everywhere. To the gratitude of hundreds of former pupils must be added the respect and admiration of all those associated with educational experiments and progress.

2. ESTABLISHMENT

As with the appointment of Meier, so with that of H. B. Jacks, it was through private canvassing of opinion, which had begun as early as 1944, that the Governors reached their decision. The new headmaster, aged 43, was on the staff of Cheltenham Junior School. He came from as unlikely a stable as his predecessor, with a Public School background and no experience of co-education. But in contrast with Meier, who was agnostic and scientific, Jacks was a committed Christian and on the arts side – though both, incidentally, were first-class hockey players. His mandate was to raise and maintain the academic standards of the school, which he succeeded in doing. His inclination was to give school life a touch more formality as regards manners and discipline: it could be said that he began by distrusting himself and what he found at the school but that he learnt to understand and love Bedales. This was in no small measure due to the support he received from his first wife, Mary, whose death in 1959 was a poignant loss to the community. 'If it were necessary,' Jacks once remarked, 'to find a single word to sum up what we are aiming at, I think I would choose the word "balance".'

Although previously intelligence tests for the admission of most pupils had been employed, it was in 1947 that more elaborate entrance tests were introduced. Candidates came to stay in the school for a couple of days and were not only given the usual intelligence tests but were also required to meet and to be taught by various members of the staff. This was a kind of junior version of Civil Service entry procedure, and great care was taken to select the boy or girl who seemed most likely to benefit from the educational experience Bedales could offer, and who possessed the degree of intelligence to do so without being under strain. Within two or three years, as the demand for places in the school increased sharply, it became necessary to turn down anything from a quarter to a half of the applicants. Lacking endowment, Bedales could offer little in the way of scholarships and bursaries. The Bedales Grant Trust Fund, founded originally in 1936, exists to provide money for bursaries, primarily, but not exclusively, for the children of O.B.s, who might find it difficult to afford to send children to Bedales. An idea of the scale of this operation can be obtained from the fact that in 1977 the cost to the school in scholarship money was £3,960, about one per cent of income from fees. Undoubtedly this policy of selection led to a noticeable change in the tone of the school in the mid-Fifties. There had arrived a core of really intelligent pupils whose abilities and tastes tended to distance them somewhat from their less academically gifted peers; this produced rifts in the homogeneity of social life, although it would be wrong to exaggerate them.

Speaking at the Diamond Jubilee of the school in 1953,

Jacks stated: 'The most important determining factor in the life of Bedales during the post-war years is to be found in the economic stringency of the times.'

By the mid-Fifties, however, the world of the Independent Schools had changed from a buyers' to a sellers' market, and that Bedales was able to take full advantage of this was owed very largely indeed to one man, Jack Walesby. He was appointed school bursar on 1 January 1948, an office which he held until December 1972, and under his skilful management the finances of Bedales were transformed. After the 'make-do and mend' policy of the war years, Walesby regularized the book-keeping system, dealt with long-standing grievances among estate employees and persuaded the Governors that the farm would never be more than a liability and must be given up. At the same time, through the wise guidance of an old friend of Bedales, H. N. Smith, the sandpit on the east side of the estate was exploited commercially, the subsequent considerable profits accruing to the school.

A key man in connection with the school's maintenance is Bill Jarman. Starting work as a lad in the early days of the Chief, he became a linchpin in the life of the school with special regard to electricity supplies when these still came from generators in the old engine-house. He met the thousand-and-one demands made on him daily by staff and pupils for the supplying or mending of gadgets. He joined in the musical and athletic life of the school and became a figure so much loved and respected that the Bedalian landscape is unthinkable without him.

The following extract from B.C. 35:6 summer 1951 gives an indication of how Bedales was evolving:

It is gratifying to reflect that Bedales was one of the pioneer progressive schools and that our system of education is being followed by an increasing number of excellent schools, some even carrying it further in the matters of freedom and independence. We are certainly justified in the pride we naturally feel, yet we must recognise that we are no longer quite the same, sturdy, self-sufficient school we were in those pioneering days. Our emphasis is shifting from the hardy manual life to broader aims of academic as well as artistic and musical achievement. I do not think that anyone, however nostalgically remembering the building in 1903 of the cricket pavilion, can seriously have regretted seeing the Memorial field built and levelled by bulldozers rather than Bedalian labour, for we must now submit to expediency and the growing pressure of the curriculum. We are compensated by our Scholarship and athletic successes for the apparent decline in constructive enthusiasm and the spirit of progressiveness that begat us. We are becoming more civilised as we grow more self-indulgent, and more productive as we slacken our grim determination to remain 'different'.

A visitor, the Rev. Ian McCulloch, is reported as saying in the *B.C.* (36:1, November 1951), 'Bedales has been breaking new ground in Ethics, in the accepted code of community life. It has discarded the conventional Ethics which leaves no room for charity in a moral judgement; but in the sphere of religious life,' he continued, 'Bedales is still backward. It needs to be more articulate in its religious experience.' He urged that dogma and religious forms are necessary to provide a pattern through which the individual can express his faith. One O.B. after another struggled, often incoherently, to defend the essentially free, albeit hazy, character of Bedalian religious experience; 'You are imposing a negative attitude,' was Mc-Culloch's counter-assertion.

In December 1956 in keeping with its traditions the school admitted two Hungarian child refugees; in 1957 the Chief took up his final residence in Fairhaven, an annexe of the Sanatorium, and became a familiar figure of affection and esteem about the school for the last ten years of his lively old age. In November 1960 Jacks presented a Memorandum to the Governors on the re-organization of Bedales into a single school for pupils from eleven-and-a-half to eighteen-and-a-half. (*See* pp. 94–6.)

One O.B. (1948–54) wrote of Jacks: 'He had the impossible task of succeeding two men of genius, and there are still some who have never forgiven him for not being a third . . . He settled down to understand Bedales and love it.' What that implied, and what helps us to comprehend the nature of Jacks' contribution to the evolution of Bedales are caught in the

The main block of the school.

The Quad seen one morning in 1978.

Steephu

Bedalians
relaxing
in the Quad.

following extracts from an article he wrote for *John Haden Badley*:

In his speech at the School Diamond Jubilee, the Chief spoke of the acorn which he had watched grow into an oak tree – but it is right to point out that a mere sixty or seventy-four years do not make a mature, fully grown oak tree . . . Someone, a good friend of Bedales – like so many, both creditor and debtor to the school—once said to me 'Bedales is my life', I knew exactly what he meant. The life-line between oneself and the school, while one is there, is a strong one. Perhaps it is best not to talk about it too much—a few steps further along the road and you may hear even if you do not heed, the familiar cry 'Bedalian arrogance'. It is interesting and perhaps a little disturbing that a place as outward going as Bedales is clearly meant to be should be so ready to turn its attention inward upon itself.

Referring to changes during his headmastership, Jacks continued:

Perhaps the simplest way of showing you the changes would be to take you up to that admirable viewpoint in the centre of the school estate, the Gym roof, and show you what you would have seen, or not have seen, in 1946 . . . We should see from there some (not all – the Steephurst bathrooms for instance would not be visible) of the outward and visible signs of progress, but the real life of the school, changing or not, would as always remain invisible; our true life lies at a great depth in us – you can see the oak tree all right, but not the life that makes it what it is. The City, said the old Greek, is the men within it, not the walls around it. Bedales is the people in it, man and woman, boy and girl . . . During the sixteen years that I was at Bedales the climate of public opinion towards co-education changed in a remarkable way: from being doubtful, critical, suspicious, even hostile, it became friendly, sympathetic and respectful. The evidence was clear and convincing. Some of the old misgivings still remain, . . . a recent article in *The Times* by a leader writer on educational subjects on the 'Possible Thinking of the Public Schools' Commission' contained this sentence: 'bizarrely enough there seems to be a strong feeling in a section of the Commission that all Public Boarding Schools should be made to become co-educational.'

Bizarre? I wonder? Oak trees have a habit, far from bizarre I should have thought, of shedding acorns.

Although their respective tenures of office as members of staff preceded and succeeded what has been called the period of establishment, this is a convenient place to put into the historical record the names of Cyril King and Joyce Caiger-Smith. The former had connections as housemaster, classics teacher and second master for forty years (1923–63); the latter as housemistress for twenty-two years (1948–70). The historical evidence reveals of Cyril King that Bedales was really his life; he loved it, and won the affection of generations of pupils for his gentle integrity, and the respect of Governors and Headmasters for his sage counsel. It reveals of Joyce Caiger-Smith that she dedicated many terms to her job and is remembered affectionately by girls who passed under her care for her own out-going and cheerful nature. The *B.C.* (55:1, autumn 1970) in an interview with 'notre dame de Steep-hurst' elicited from her the following remark: 'One of the things that I feel about Bedales is that any crisis brings out the best every time and I almost welcome such things as the 'flu epidemics.'

3. EXPANSION

Unlike the previous two appointments, the third, of T. W. Slack, was made by the Governors after public advertisement of the vacancy. (Slack was 34, and headmaster of Kambawsa School, Burma.) It had become clear to the Governors that for a variety of reasons, some of them economic and some of them educational, it would be in the best interest of the school for it to increase its numbers (*see* Appendix III). Appointed, though not exclusively so, with this consideration in mind, Slack carried through successfully the task with which he had been entrusted, namely to expand the school's numbers. In a message from the Governors and the headmaster the objectives were succinctly described and an appeal for £150,000 was launched. As these objectives were largely attained by the time of Slack's retirement in 1974, they can be conveniently summarized in the words of the original statement of them:

What do we want to do and why do we want to do it?

(i)   A greater range of activities for a wide spread of ability:

We want to make sure that all boys and girls have full opportunity to develop their potential to its full and experience at some point in their school lives a sense of achievement.

A rise in numbers from two hundred and forty to three hundred and forty at Bedales will allow for better grouping up to 'O' Level in subjects where classes need to be divided according to ability. In particular the workshop and art school need to work together and provide facilities appropriate for contemporary life such as engineering, technical drawing, fabric printing, design etc. The provision of more technical activities will tie together and make relevant skills learnt in the Science Department and Workshop.

(ii)   A Larger Sixth Form:

We believe that Bedales should be a school where all can continue their education with advantage up to the age of eighteen. To provide a vigorous and extensive final two years we need a much larger Sixth Form. The increase in size will come partly from the increased numbers lower down the school, and partly from a direct entry at Sixth Form level. This new entry for a two-year course should open Bedales to many who do not want or cannot afford a longer period. It also gives new scope for increasing the international in-take into the school. We need not only to make provision for possible new subjects like Economics, but also to have more pupils in groups that are at present undersized. The provision of two sets in some subjects will allow greater flexibility of approach and some increase of choice. We must give a better Sixth Form education to those not aiming at Universities, thus encouraging all pupils irrespective of their academic ability to remain at Bedales until they are eighteen.

(iii)   More places for Day pupils:

Since education is aimed at preparing people to live effectively in the world, we should avoid the dangers of too cloistered an existence which a school that is exclusively boarding can create. We need to mix more with the neighbourhood and work more in the local community. Moreover, we hope that vacancies for more Day pupils will enable us to accept children from a wider financial background.

(iv)   Change the age of entry:

We wish to fit in more with the requirements of a growing number of parents and, in order to integrate more effectively with points of transfer, in the State system, we plan to have multiple points of entry at nine, eleven, thirteen and Sixth Form level.

(v)   Smaller house units:

We need to give more individual attention than is possible in the present two-House system, which has already become stretched to unwieldy limits as the school has grown to its present size of two hundred and forty.

(vi)   Better staff accommodation:

This matter needs urgent attention if we are to continue to recruit and retain staff of high quality.

(vii)   Improvement of existing facilities:

The Assembly Hall is too small for the present size of the school. Dining arrangements are most unsatisfactory. Senior boys and girls badly need a study area with individual places. Sports facilities need improvement.

(viii)   Making the school a more viable financial unit:

Although the reasons for this development programme are primarily educational and social, a moderate increase in numbers will help us to contain the ever rising costs.

In spite of admiration for the deft way in which Slack carried out the expansion exercise, some natural doubts were expressed during the Sixties as to the degree to which Bedales would be able to keep its distinctive flavour and identity. The rise in numbers, the new Sixth Form entry which meant a considerable portion of the seniors coming from other kinds of school without roots in the Bedalian tradition, and the inevitable rise in fees: might not the combination of these factors tend to make it more of a rich man's establishment than previously? The nature of this concern is well caught by quoting a couple of extracts of self-assessment from the *B.C.* (48:2, spring 1964):

Few who know anything about Bedales today still think of it as a 'crank school'; it is known for sending good historians to Oxford, good musicians to the National Youth Orchestra, good doctors and engineers all over the world and even good actresses to Hollywood. It has been considered suitable for the sisters of Etonians, younger brothers bullied at Worksop and those whose seams have grown too tight at Dartington. In short, Bedalian values and methods have become respectable.

Yet the second extract, referring to a 'central paradox', points to a 'contradiction between the internal values of Bedales and its relationship to the outward world'. At the 1968 Bedales Company summer meeting Professor Donnison, associated with the governmental commission of enquiry into Independent Schools, was invited to speak on 'The Education Rat-Race and its Effect on Bedales School'.

As the Seventies approached a certain discontent could be sensed inside the school; there were a few drinking and drugs incidents, and the tentacles of the permissive society in the world outside began to fasten somewhat on to the school community. And yet Bedales provided a handsome picture of exceptionally flourishing music, outstanding academic performance and a truly remarkable richness of cultural activity.

Writing in *John Haden Badley*, Gyles Brandreth (1961–6) commented:

Bedales is no longer a Cause. It is an established, a fashionable, a successful institution that no longer needs to crusade. The pioneering spirit so evident in the earlier years has vanished, and with it has gone much of the sense of commitment to the progressive ideal in education. Nevertheless, Bedales is a better school now than it was three-quarters of a century ago. I am inclined to think it is a better school now than it has ever been. But there are those who disagree . . . Nonetheless, as an American headmaster said to me not long ago at the National Association

D

of Independent Schools Convention in New York, 'Can you show me a better Boarding School in the British Isles?' It all depends on what you are looking for, but I cannot.

However intangible this may sound, the *Times Educational Supplement* wrote at the time of the Chief's one hundredth birthday, 'There is an atmosphere at Bedales unlike any other Independent School in a sense of maturity, of self-respect, of co-operation and common purpose, without the awkwardness or self-conscious heartiness of a Public School . . . In the Sixties Bedales grumbled and yet remained a very happy place.'
    Mr Slack has himself supplied an apt comment:

Mr. Badley once told me of a boy whom he admitted into the school at the age of seventeen. After a few weeks when it became clear that he was not doing very well, the boy admitted that he was nineteen – having felt previously that the claim to be over seventeen satisfied his conscience. The Badley solution was generous and typically unorthodox – he switched the boy onto the staff. I applaud the spirit and spontaneity which lay behind this action, but know that the necessarily more structured form of the school which has been with us for some time would today prevent such Quixotic actions. Whether we like it or not, the demand to make the life for those in the school relevant to the life which they are going to lead having left school, leads to a far higher degree of planning for the future than was necessary in the past.

In that last sentence there lies perhaps a clue to the nature of the special and distinguished contribution which this fourth headmaster made to the evolution of the school.

4. ON COURSE

It is no business of the historian to intrude upon the present, so this last section is appropriately brief. The present head-master, Patrick Nobes, who was appointed at the age of 41 after the vacancy had once again been publicly advertised, was previously headmaster of a Comprehensive school.
    As on previous occasions H.M. Inspectors found a great deal to admire in Bedales during their visits in 1976 and 1977. It

is fitting that the last words of this section of the history of Bedales should be those of its present headmaster: 'My main hope for the future is that for as long as it is necessary, and in a not unprogressive way, we retain this school as a bee in amber for the present generation of schools and people in education to observe.'

CHAPTER SEVEN

The Dunhurst Story

★

It is easy to understand how Dunhurst emerged, not by any means as a mere appendage of the Bedales Secondary School, but developing over the years a validity and identity of its own. An account of its origin, written in 1946, has been given by its first headmaster, Mr Russell Scott, who joined the Bedales staff when the school moved in 1900 from Sussex to its new site:

My invaluable adjutant throughout was Miss Borsche who had been trained at the Pestalozzi–Froebel Haus, and she was proposed to me by Mr. and Mrs. Badley with whom she had been living in charge of their little Jock where she was fully in touch with Bedales life.

Dunhurst developed in September 1902 out of the class of little boys and girls that was formed at the Upper school when I urged that the constant trouble with these children was due to the error of our own belief that all ages should be combined as in a family. We came to see that the nine year olds should not be expected to adapt themselves to a succession of specialist teachers, but should get to feel at home with a single person, a Jack of all trades. For that job I was perhaps picked because of what Mr. Badley long afterwards kindly called my versatility. It was the success of this experiment that indicated its extension to separate living conditions. It was far from being assumed that this extension should be confided to me; but that was the ultimate decision, and even then it was only by chance that the building of a school could be done with capital brought in by me at a time when the growth of the Upper school (which had no library or swimming bath) had a use for all Mr. Badley's capital. Except that the appointment of my staff was thus purely my own affair I felt no change in my relations with my headmaster. He remained my

Chief, and a suggestion from him would have had almost the force of a command; but only once in these ten years did he make one. It was when a certain incident caused him to say that he thought more supervision was needed of the free time spent by the children in the open grounds. When I left and went to America he had no financial difficulty in 1912 in taking over the school, but he did not at all welcome the opportunity. 'Must this thing be?' he said to me wistfully. 'Absolutely, yes,' I replied.

At first a handful of children were taught in a garden hut of the Russell Scotts' house, Hillcroft, in Steep, but by 1905 a new purpose-built block had been erected on the south-west portion of the Bedales estate. When Russell Scott left, he was succeeded, after a term's interregnum under Mr and Mrs Murray Williams, by Mr Epps. He remained until he went off to the First World War in 1917, by which time the Senior/ Junior school link, with separate headmasters but working as a joint concern, had been established.

Since its establishment Dunhurst has passed through three discernible eras: 1917–39 under Mrs S. C. Fish; 1939–54 under Miss Amy Clarke; and the years since then under five head-masters and with the addition to it in 1953 of a pre-preparatory school. Its relationship to the senior school at Bedales has been a varied one, never altogether isolated from it, but, considering its physical proximity, curiously and sometimes awkwardly remote from it.

This was not so at the beginning of the first era: Mrs Fish was a close friend of Badley's with no educational training whatever but with immense respect for the Chief and an in-tuitive grasp of what young children require, who are growing up away from home in a boarding school environment. She herself, writing in the *B.C.* Jubilee Number, remarked:

I accepted the Headship of Dunhurst almost accidentally, to fill a sudden vacancy in the middle of a term. I took on the post with misgivings. For the past six years I had lived with my own boy in a house on the outskirts of Petersfield, and had taken into my home a little group of other children. The ages of the children varied from three to twelve. As their parents lived abroad, the children stayed with me throughout the whole year. As I had never had any training as a teacher, I wisely did not attempt to teach, but was fortunate in obtaining the help of a gifted, cultured woman who came daily to teach the children . . . it was much later that I realised to some extent at least we had shown that, given right conditions, it was possible for children to lead a simple and natural home life, and to attain, without factitious pressures, rewards or punishments, the ordinary standard of learning considered necessary for children of their age. I was prepared for many difficulties when I went to Dunhurst. What I had not realised was the tremendous handicap with which I started, in never having lived in a school. Looking back I feel I began my work with only one asset – I knew what I wanted . . . everything seemed wrong with the school. Here were some thirty normal children, boys and girls, between the ages of seven and thirteen, held down by rigid discipline, occupied, but unsatisfied, discontented and rebellious. At last help came. Some years earlier, while still living in Petersfield, I had read the newly published work of Dr. Montessori, and, through the Chief, had been put in touch with Miss Clarke who had studied under the Dottoressa in Rome and Barcelona. During an O.B. meeting, she came to see me, and although her visit lasted barely half an hour I knew instantly that in her I had found the ideal teacher. My first impulse after I had accepted the post at Dunhurst was to get in touch with her and beg for her help. But this offer, repeated many times, was persistently refused. It was only when her health broke down and she was compelled to give up her slum work in London that she agreed to work in the school. From that day life changed. Dunhurst became a living, sentient project, filled with promise . . . Something was essential for the wellbeing of the children : if the Chief agreed, and there was money in the bank, help was forthcoming. If not, a young and enthusiastic staff were called together, and plans were made to earn the money for the building. Both the Barn and the Workshop were built and equipped in this way.

A chance meeting with the venerable musician at Haslemere, Arnold Dolmetsch, roused his interest in the school. He came, and the children conquered him. For six years he and his children visited and taught in the school. At one time, in a school of sixty children, forty were learning String instruments.

With Miss Clarke as her head teacher, Mrs Fish struck the keynote of Dunhurst education during this first era: absence of 'factitious pressures', strong, sometimes autocratic direction from the top, but such an atmosphere of sweetness and light as would have pleased the heart of Matthew Arnold; it won the devotion of generations of Dunhurstians.

The second era (1939–54) under the dedicated headmistress-ship of Miss Clarke carried on this tradition and was blessed with a permanence of staffing, which gave remarkable stability to the school. Where there were so many admirable and lovable characters, it is invidious to select only some for mention, but their colleagues must be forgiving if the only ones mentioned here are Mr Tilley, later to run successfully a school of his own, Miss Cocker (later Mrs Messingham) whose genius lay in the art of making mathematics enjoyable as well as comprehensible, Miss Cormack, with her Barn which linked Dunhurst and Bedales children in a common love of craft, and Mr Messingham (Chips) and his Workshop. One of his old pupils referred to him affectionately as 'crazy enough to assume that boys and girls of eleven could do first-class cabinet work. I doubt whether I have learnt anything as important since.'

Another Old Dunhurstian writes:

In especial affection I remember the Dunhurst Workshop under Mr. Messingham. The whole atmosphere of the wooden building filled with warm wooden shapes – benches – tools – supplies etc. (all used, worn, loved, silted in shavings despite sweepings up) and the old linseed oil pots with worn down, gummed up shabby brushes, for dabbing on saws and planes – the pots with an age old build-up of dry oil, and Mr. Messingham's love for his craft and the respect he tried to teach for the tools: these certainly stayed with me, and second to my painting (as a professional artist) I love to create things out of wood, I enjoy wood as a medium and natural substance.

In *John Haden Badley*, a later headmaster has managed to evoke the special Dunhurst atmosphere:

Cor's light [Miss Cormack, teacher of craft] has been shining out late into the night from the Barn since 1929 with the constancy of a good deed in a naughty world . . . lucky the child who learnt Mathematics from Mrs. Messingham's neat basket (in which everything was 'according to Cocker') or who was given food for a life-time's laughter – and even speculation? – by being sent by Mr. Messingham [teacher of woodwork] to 'collect some holes' for the egg rack he was making.

In September 1953 a pre-preparatory school for day children was opened at Dunannie, an old farmhouse with fields attached on the west side of the Petersfield/Steep road; it had recently been purchased by Bedales. With the age of admission to Dunhurst raised to about seven-and-a-half, Dunannie catered for the four-and-a-half to seven-and-a-half age group, for its first twenty years under the wise and lovable headmistress-ship of Sophie Tatchell and subsequently under that of her distinguished successor, Mrs Mellish. When the Dunannie buildings were sold, the pre-preparatory section moved into part of the Dunhurst building.

The third era of Dunhurst has been passed under five headmasters, Stephen Hogg (1954–7), Paul Townsend (1957–64), Douglas Juckes (1964–70), Philip Pike (1970–4), and, since 1974, Alastair Langlands. The main features of these years have been: first, the preservation of the original Dunhurst atmosphere of loving care for young children, accompanied by steadily rising academic standards; second, a structural re-organization, which was marked by the establishment in September 1970 of a Middle School with entry at eleven and the principle gradually adopted of no boarders at Dunhurst under the age of nine. Entry at eleven was at first favoured by the Governors as being likely to solve administrative problems already defined by Paul Townsend as those of 'a non-selective primary school at the tail-end of a Grammar School'. It was also seen as a movement in line with the state sector towards providing a particular kind of schooling suitable for the age group nine to thirteen or fourteen, which could be thought of as having outgrown primary and not yet being ready for full secondary education.

The first master-in-charge was Mr G. Pearson. A member of the Dunhurst staff since 1967, it was he who experimented in the Middle School Blocks 1 and 2 with Nuffield Science,

and Data Processing Systems and Work-Cards. However, the
dual system of control consisting of a headmaster at Dunhurst
and a master-in-charge of the Middle School proved unsatisfactory, and so after succeeding Pearson as master-in-charge
of the Middle School in September 1973, Alastair Langlands
became headmaster of both in September 1974. The admission
ages then became four-and-a-half at Dunannie, nine at Dunhurst, eleven at Middle School and thirteen at Bedales.

Undoubtedly the most attractive feature of this re-structured
age-grouping is that the Junior schools are totally free from
examination pressure between four-and-a-half and thirteen:
and yet only three children failed to pass on to the Senior
School in the last three years. This has enabled an admirable
balance to be struck between acquisition of skills in the three
Rs (about fifty per cent of time available) and a host of other
activities including field camps for the Middle School (the
other fifty per cent). In a pamphlet, timed for publication at
the seventy-fifth anniversary of the founding of Dunhurst, its
present headmaster has picked out as its six salient characteristics: principles, practice, community, love, excellence,
lightness of touch. Their outward signs are apparent in an
account of the school's activities during the year 1975–6:

Several local schools spent a day in the Sports Hall performing
The Moonrakers, a dramatic piece for choir, orchestra and mime;
for Christmas 1975 there was a performance of *The Tailor of
Gloucester*, written largely by Alexandra Harwood, aged ten and
a half, and realised by Dunhurst and Middle School pupils; another
joint production in the Spring was *Mac the Sheep Stealer*, a
musical version of the Second Wakefield Shepherd's Play. Both
were performed in the Quad. In Steep Church (where several
pupils have sung regularly in the Matins Choir) for Easter the
Middle School performed another Miracle Play, *The Crucifixion*;
and, for Christmas 1976, *Wackie and his Fuddlegee* was played in
the Sports Hall by Dunhurst. Musical composition among Dunhurst pupils has flourished and some of the pupils' classwork has
been closely linked with drama.

Middle School has done much construction work at the Single-
ton Open Air Museum; the Summer Field Study Camps were held
beneath a cloudless sky at Glastonbury and Bembridge. Dunhurst

D*

Group 4 camped and walked the last miles of the Pilgrim's Way before acting the murder of Becket in the crypt of Canterbury Cathedral as a finale to their medieval studies.

The school proudly received the British Heart Foundation's Shield for having the most sponsors in a swim which raised hundreds of pounds for research.

CHAPTER EIGHT

Hand, Heart, Head, Hunch

★

Earth, water, air, fire; sensation, emotion, thought, intuition; perhaps it is the exceptionally successful blending of these four elements and four human qualities which provides the key to life at Bedales.

I. HAND AND HEART

If Aesthetics has been rightly described as the 'science of sensuous knowledge', then Bedales has been a consistent practitioner of it. Indeed one O.B. goes so far as to write: 'The most singular achievement of the school, I consider, was to give everyone a very wide appreciation of the Arts – Ronald Biggs [Director of Bedales music for many years] was the brilliant Antony Hopkins of our day – and this may be the most special thing that Bedales offered.'

Not only in music, but in drama, workshop, studio and outdoor work, pupils and staff followed the pursuit of sensuous knowledge and were fortunate enough to do so in a setting of great natural beauty. Five hundred different wild flowers have been counted between the villages of Steep and Froxfield: in his poem, 'May the twenty-third', Edward Thomas immortalized 'Old Jack Noman's cresses from Oakshott Rill and his cowslips from Wheatham Hill'. The countryside in which Bedales lies has exercised its spell over successive generations of pupils – a fact most tellingly illustrated by the number of their loving (and just occasionally loathing) references to it and to their Expeds. into it on Sundays, especially in the school's early days. The balance between human beings and their environment is a delicate one, the former often decisively influenced by the latter. In this case Badley's own eye for natural beauty – he himself was an enthusiastic and not un-skilful painter in water colours – together with the emphasis placed from the outset on the community leading an active, outdoor life, must in themselves have helped.

Outdoor work has had its fat and lean years, but it has remained a fairly constant feature of school life. Its *raison d'être* has been a compound of two factors: first, sheer necessity to mobilize manpower in the pioneering days, for such a project as the levelling of the top cricket pitch and on the farm during the two wars; but second, a conviction that frequent actual physical contact with nature is a pedagogical necessity, that by cutting and sawing wood, or collecting up leaves, a kind of virtue can enter into the workers conducive to fellow feeling. Whether your partner at the other end of a two-handed saw is boyfriend or girlfriend, athlete or scholar, member of staff or headmaster, the relationship necessarily set up between the partners permits of no escape from honesty of human exchange.

The 'Workshop' at Bedales conjures up three names: Captain Taylor, the chief though not the only teacher of handicraft in the early part of this century; 'Biff' Barker, whose undisputed reign lasted with one gap of four years from 1922 to 1964; and his illustrious successor David Butcher, who, as head of the Design Department, has pioneered an imaginative 'O' Level course which links art and craft with mathematics, history, economics and the everyday world. As H. B. Jacks wrote in *John Haden Badley*:

Practical work of every kind has always played a large part both in the curriculum and in general esteem at Bedales. We regard what many schools still speak of as out-of-school activities or extras (woodwork, metalwork, handicraft generally) as of equal educational value with any other subject in the school curriculum, and it is for their own intrinsic and educational value these activities are given such prominence in the life of the school, far more than for any practical benefit that they might bring to the school. It is hardly surprising that so many of the school buildings and some of its equipment bear the touch of great craftsmen's hands or that there are many names on the School Roll that are well-known wherever good craftsmanship is appreciated.

Two examples are Edward Barnsley C.B.E., famous for his furniture making, and Roger Powell for his bookbinding (including the Book of Kells and the restoration of books in Florence after the flooding of 1966). An impressive and moving tribute comes from Tanya Drawbridge (née Ashkin), sculptress and silversmith :

At Bedales I lived in the workshop, discovering metal-work too, and eventually training as a silversmith when I left school. The staff saw that I was serious in my interest and encouraged me in every way. They even commissioned me to make a silver bowl for the Chief's 90th Birthday as their present to him. Biff Barker collected the money for it and bought me a collection of tools as payment. I still have all the tools and use and cherish them. Perhaps of historical interest would be the Bedales Hallmark. When I was thirteen I made two silver pieces, a sugar spoon and a trinket box for my parents' Silver Wedding. Professor Hutton, one of the School Governors, was a member of the Goldsmiths' Hall, and he suggested that I apply for my own Hallmark. I did this, and within the next two years two other pupils, Robert Jeffcock and Paul Thompson also got Hallmarks. Although I went on to study silversmithing seriously, it was realised that anyone making a silver bowl, instead of a copper or gilded metal one, could apply for a Hallmark, and then never use it again. So Bedales itself acquired its own Hallmark for any Bedalian to use.

Perhaps the most splendid feature of the workshop was that it was open and available for individual and collective use all day every day.

The same feature of openness and availability applies to the Studio, which has always played a vital part in the life of the school. The teaching of art at Bedales has attracted gifted staff – Innes Meo, Nommie Durrell and Christopher Cash, to mention only three. A letter from the second of these conveys the flavour of art at Bedales:

Though I may have had better and more erudite results since I left Bedales, due to progress in myself, it was at Bedales that I had the most enjoyable teaching because the school seems to attract a rather special sort of pupil. I followed after a very special sort of teacher, Innes Meo, [known as Gi-gi] – very fortunately I met him later on and counted him among my friends. His unique gifts and endearing personality were a very valuable influence in the school to the children and the staff alike, and they all loved him.

When I started teaching at Bedales it was soon after Gi-gi, and he was then a rich legend – my approach to Art teaching may have been different, but we arrived at the same result, that is, Art . . . I think that there were two main events during my time, firstly, Sir Herbert Read publishing his book *Education Through Art*, illustrated by paintings from Bedales and in some measure drawing on my work, . . . the second event was an exhibition of Bedales' paintings which I arranged with Major Lasson at his Beaux Arts Gallery in Breton Place.

Michael Wishart O.B. has paid the following tribute:

My first exhibition in London was held when I was just sixteen, in fact still at school. It was a great success and one of the happiest events in my life. All my paintings are silently dedicated to Mrs. Durrell, who taught me at Bedales.

Throughout its history Bedales has always played games without making a fetish of them. Soccer, Rugger, cricket, hockey, tennis, fives, squash – all these have had their place and owe the pleasure they have given to so many hundreds of Bedalians in very large measure to one man, H. E. W. Bennett ('Benn'). Appointed by Badley as groundsman and coach, he became during his twenty-one years on the staff very much more than that. At one stage he and his wife ran the overflow boarding house of Lithcott, and it was largely he and a few enthusiastic cricketers who in 1934 founded the Stoner Cricket Club: for many summers the Stoner Cricket Week has been a fixture, with enjoyable matches played between O.B.s and a variety of local teams.

In recent years an annual event has been the Le Mans Cycle Race, in which the participants compete lap after lap around the school grounds and generate tremendous enthusiasm and competitiveness. One of the quaint and most endearing features of Bedales life, which certainly requires a mention in any account of the science of sensuous knowledge, are the Room-doers. They handle most of the school's furniture-shifting and have evolved over the years their own lumbering, but digni-fied, mystique!

The two most substantial features of aesthetic life at Bedales have undoubtedly been music and drama. Since the days of Ma B. and Osbos, music has played an ever-increasing role in the school. The names associated with the teaching and foster-ing of it make an impressive list, from Sir John Steuart Wilson via Harry Platts, Nancy Strudwick and William Agnew, to the present Director of Music, Jonathan Willcocks, but the one which stands out from them all is that of Ronald Biggs. In the capacity of Director or Adviser he was associated with Bedales from 1923 to 1967, and in *John Haden Badley* he paints a rich canvas of Bedalian musical activities:

In 1923, if my memory serves, the 'orchestra' consisted of a few strings, one flute and a piano. Eight years later the orchestra had advanced to such a point that it was able to combine with singers from Frensham Heights and perform a work by Hinde-mith at the International Festival of Contemporary Music which took place in England that year. In the meantime, what had been the girls' gym was converted into a music school with about a dozen practice rooms. Not ideal, but a great advance on leaking wooden huts and practice pianos under the stage in Lupton Hall. A van-load of decaying pianos departed and were replaced by new ones. Bedales now had at least some musical equipment. In 1932 I too departed to direct music at Dartington Hall where I met Harry Platts, who agreed to take my place at Bedales. For nine years he cherished and inspired Bedales music with the greatest devotion and skill. When I retired from the B.B.C. Bedales asked me to return in 1947 as part-Director. Soon after that Bedales gave a B.B.C. broadcast, which at that time was more unusual than it might be now. This included Whole School Singing, the Orchestra, a number of soloists and some Chamber music. And about that time the choir recorded some Vaughan Williams in the film series 'March of Time'. I shall never forget the first per-formance ever given in the Quad, Purcell's *Dido and Aeneas*. The sun beat down through the glass roof and the Quad became an oven . . .

For many years it was possible to maintain a String Quartet on the music staff, and Chamber music was thriving. We instituted exchange concerts with other schools, Bryanston, Charterhouse, Eton and the longstanding yearly visit to Horndean Music Club.

An important landmark was the building at a cost of some £15,000 of the new music school, which was formally opened in 1960 by the Principal of the Royal Academy of Music: at that time one hundred and sixty-one pupils out of a school total of some three hundred and fifty were learning instruments. Music was played at Assembly (whole school morning or evening gatherings) and on Sunday evenings when outside players and singers would also perform from time to time. Several Bedalians were selected to play in the National Youth Orchestra, and others have made a great reputation for themselves as instrumental soloists: they include Peter Graeme, Gervais de Peyer and Martin Birnstingl.

Drama has been as important as music, and Bedales has concerned itself with two types of drama. One is the rehearsed performing of a play primarily for the play's sake and for the experience it gives pupils of acting a variety of adult parts; the other is the pedagogical use of drama for pupils' self-expression, very often through improvisation exercises. Originally the two tended to get confused: little so-and-so would be given the part of Macbeth because it would be good for him, bring him out, pretty well regardless of standards of production and performance. Gradually, however, this error has been rectified, nowhere more so than at Bedales, where a correct distinction between the functions of these two modes of drama is preserved.

Three names are most frequently associated with drama at Bedales, Geoffrey Crump, Rachel Carey Field and, in a different genre, Basil Gimson. The first of these, reputed to have produced or acted in over fifty or sixty plays during his time at Bedales, had to strive hard to establish the distinction described above, but he succeeded in so doing and vastly improved the standard of oral work through speech training and the practice of choric speech. A Dramatic Society has flourished; there have been Senior and Junior Dramatic Competitions; interest has been continued amongst O.B.s, who used to put on their own productions at O.B. meetings and co-operate with Crump in his productions of Shakespeare in the gardens of Lord Horder at Ashford Chase.

Gimmy's Gilbert & Sullivan productions provided immense enjoyment and the outlet for many different kinds of pupil talent. From time to time the school orchestra would need reinforcing by what came to be known as 'the wind from Portsmouth', three or four professional wind instrumentalists – always welcome but presenting a nice problem for housemaster and housemistress: namely how to prevent the beer the musicians required for their efforts from reaching unlawful destinations! The two productions which linger most vividly in my own memory of the Thirties are Shaw's *St Joan* and Eliot's *Murder in the Cathedral*. In the former Mary Goodland was the Maid, infinitely moving and dramatic, Piers Plowman the Dauphin, Gimmy the Inquisitor and Geoffrey Crump the Earl of Warwick; not to mention a lovely backcloth for the river scene painted by Gi-gi and his helpers. In the latter there was the first really splendid piece of choric speaking at Bedales by the Women of Canterbury and a very fine performance by Arnold Polak in the part of Becket.

Under Rachel Carey Field (1941–75) a unique theatrical wardrobe was built up and a whole series of memorable productions mounted under her talented and sensitive production. In 1958 a special display panel of Bedales work was included by the British Drama League in their selection of photographs sent to an International Exhibition at Seattle. Harold Gardiner, head of English between 1952 and 1968, won the deep esteem and affection of his pupils, and caught the spirit of Bedales drama in an article he wrote for the *B.C.* (52:3, summer 1958):

At the O.B., sixteen years ago, on a weekend of thunder and lightning which cut off the electricity, I first experienced a Bedales play. That night it was *The Lady's not for Burning*, and I went home in a mood somewhat like Keats after reading Chapman. This was school drama beyond anything I had thought possible.

In front of me as I write is a copy of the programme for *Pillars of Society* (December 1951) – printed as always by the Bedales Press, to whom I would like to pay a tribute for their craftsmanship and co-operation through the years. On this programme are numerous autographs, mostly accompanied by 'with love from' or 'lots of love' or followed by lavish use of kisses. These tell the story of the very special kind of tolerance, and the sinking of self in the corporate activity which can be bred by school plays. Many of us must have realised, while we watched rehearsals, that working together had made the cast, the stage-hands, the props. and wardrobe people, the tape-recorder operators into people of finer feelings and understanding.

Other memorable productions at Bedales included *Peer Gynt* (1946), *Hamlet* (1958). *Cockpit* (1960), *The Winter's Tale* (1971) and the musical, *Phineas Finn* (1976).

II. HEAD AND HUNCH

Mind and spirit have always been closely intertwined at Bedales; lessons in the classroom, reading in the library, Jaws in the Lupton Hall and day-to-day socializing in the Quad, these have constituted the *genius loci*. It is incidentally of interest to speculate what effect on social cohesion was made by the removal of the classrooms from the central school building to the estate outside. Did it, as one O.B. maintains, result in the Quad becoming a more or less 'male Steephurst?'

In many ways the Bedales classrooms differed little from those in most other schools – same subjects, generally though not always studied in orthodox ways, same desks and tables and chairs and blackboards, and yet in reality very different indeed because of the small numbers in each class, often less than twenty, the individual attention paid to each child, the enthusiasm of the majority of teachers to communicate their knowledge and skills and the lack of inhibition among the pupils in asking questions. During the early Thirties a considerable amount of pioneering work went on under Kenneth Barnes (1930–40) in what was to become known nationally as General Science. This itself was a legacy of two outstanding masters of scientific pedagogical method, Charles Vernon (1924–30) and Eric Rogers (1928–30). It reached a climax with the brilliant teaching of F. A. Meier himself during his own headmastership.

Various O.B.s have commented on the 'wonderful opportunities not to work' and the 'arbitrary dropping of subjects'. Certainly, until well into the Fifties there were strong and conflicting arguments between staff and pupils as to just how much academic pressure was compatible with free development in a pupil's own time. After that date the balance began to swing in the direction of academic pressures, but every attempt continued to be made to preserve the sanctity of the other criteria of each child's own timely growth.

Joan King, herself an O.B. and member of staff at two periods, remarked in *John Haden Badley*:

In spite of the changes which a changing world has brought to teaching at Bedales, I think that up to now a feeling of individual responsibility for one's own progress has been kept. There is still an emphasis on learning, rather than on being taught. I feel very strongly that this emphasis is largely due to the library, with its carefully guarded tradition of unsupervised work and silence. This tradition, which we take almost for granted, but which visitors find so impressive, has had an abiding influence on the teaching at Bedales.

Indeed it has, and on more than the teaching: 'I think,' one sixth former is quoted as saying in the *Hampshire County Magazine* of May 1958, 'it is the most religious place in the school.' Completed as a War Memorial in 1921, 'the library,' writes one O.B., 'was quite a social milieu despite its rule of silence: eye contact and note-writing went on, and its rather open structure with a balcony level made it quite a theatre.' Yes, that was so, for romance and scholarship, serenity and fun are always haunting those oak-lined window-bays.

The librarian from 1926 to 1958 was Barbara Crump, under whose loving care the number of books rose from 7,000 to 22,000; by 1972 it exceeded 30,000. She and her successors not only fostered the skills of librarianship among pupils by training many of them as assistants, but also acted as guardians of a sanctuary and power-house of scholarship in the school.

The spiritual link between the library and Jaw is aptly illustrated in the following poem which Rabindranath Tagore wrote on the occasion of his visit to Bedales in July 1920, and which was subsequently on display:

Speak to Me of Him

> Speak to him of me, my friend, and say that
> he has whispered to you in the hushed centre
> of fight and in the depth of peace where life
> puts on its armour. Shrink not to call his
> name in the crowd, for we need to turn our eyes
> to the heart of things, to see the vision of
> truth and love building the world anew out of
> its wreckage.
> Speak to me, my friend of him, and make it
> simple for me to feel that he is.

What passed in the quiet hours of the library and in the meditation of Jaw did indeed make it simple for many a Bedalian to feel 'that he is'.

From earliest days there have been regular Sunday evening services: their form was prescribed by Badley himself and consists of prayers, hymns, readings and addresses, mostly expressed in Christian terminology but without dogmatism or denominational assertion and capable of offering a platform for any speaker concerned with human values. Badley's own contribution can be studied in a collection of his Jaws entitled *These make Men's Lives*.* After his retirement more outside speakers were invited to speak, as well as members of staff, and a very wide range of topics was handled, particularly in the socio-political field.

It is difficult to interpret the evidence regarding the significance of this feature of Bedales life. Although undoubtedly there must have been occasions of boredom and inattention, not surprising perhaps considering the wide age range of pupils and staff, two deep and positive impressions remain. One is the fact that this coming together of the whole community at a regular time in the week, which was almost always graced with beautiful music, has served as a spiritual cement. The second is the fact that individual Bedalians have recorded how on various occasions they have been moved in the depths of their being and often for a lifetime.

Sir Selwyn Selwyn-Clarke, K.B.E., C.M.G., M.C. (Bedales 1905) has recalled how, as a prisoner-of-war in the hands of

* Oxford: Blackwell, 1935.

the Japanese during the Second World War, he felt that he could almost hear the Chief's voice saying the prayer at the end of Sunday Jaw, 'May they feel that Thy loving care is ever with them in all their troubles and perplexities so that they may come safe through every danger;' words, absorbed in youth, full of hope and solace for a prisoner.

Another recollection is that of Professor John MacMurray, speaking one Sunday evening shortly before the outbreak of World War II, to an audience much troubled in its heart and mind: 'I congratulate you,' he began, 'on being fortunate enough to live at this time when the prospects of human freedom are greater than ever before': the school's morale soared. Finally, there was Max Plowman ending a Jaw about Joan of Arc by remarking, 'I think a saint is born every time anyone forgives an enemy.'

Dormitory life on the Boys' Flat and with the girls at Steephurst has undoubtedly always played an important part in determining the quality of existence at Bedales. This is a result of the strenuously maintained practice of having mixed-age groups in small units of four to eight with a 'Boss' in charge of each bedroom. The amount and quality of caring displayed by older boys and girls for the younger ones, the avoidance, with a few exceptions, of bullying, the sensible poking fun at undue extremes of hairstyle, make-up or dress, and the intimate discussion of emotional relationships between peers and between seniors and juniors have been commented on with deep appreciation by succeeding generations of pupils. Criticism has arisen from time to time on the ground of the lack of privacy in the day-to-day design for living. Originally there was literally nowhere for individuals to enjoy solitude; such facilities have recently become more available, but it may still be true to suggest that there is a premium set on gregariousness.

At various times in the school's history, different experiments in degrees of self-government have been attempted, ranging from a traditional prefectorial system with Head Boy and Head Girl, to consultative government by means of a School Council consisting of pupils and staff with ultimate control, however, remaining in the hands of the headmaster,

and Collective Responsibility, which implied general sixth-
form supervision of school discipline and social organization.

It seems as though, beginning in the Fifties and increasing in
the mid-Sixties, there was a detectable movement towards
much greater sophistication of mind and manners in the
school:

Because there was always so much going on at Bedales with
(relatively) so few to take part, each Bedalian had to become 'a
universal man' to some extent. Non-musical pupils learnt to play
instruments because (1) it was done (2) there was excellent tuition
(3) players were needed for the various orchestras.

Very important was the tone set by the sophisticated London
Jews – how knowledgeable they seemed to the Provincial Gentile.
They created a spirit of cultural emulation, which came from
below, not from the staff – Glyndebourne was the name to con-
jure with, not Arsenal . . . The prestige of art, of music and of
asceticism in life and work (in dress and estate work) can hardly
be over-emphasised as values among the pupils. Nobody, even the
nouveaux riches, had any pocket money to speak of: there was no
living it up beyond a little cider. The original cult or myth of the
school as it was in 1900 kept perpetually reviving among the
leading spirits of the pupils. It had not become an ordinary
school. [O.B. boy of the Fifties.]

On the other hand an O.B. boy of the Sixties has noted a
change to 'bright, competitive, get-on kids' – reflecting the
change from a buyers' to a sellers' market in the economy of
pupil entry to Independent schools. He comments further on
the economic, social and intellectual élitism of Bedales in the
mid-Sixties: 'We were trained as super heads, not super
people.'

What of co-education? The first point to make is that, after
the initial shock of its introduction, it has become a normal
feature of the Bedalian way of life. Sexual promiscuity has
never been a feature, although sexual experiment and ex-
ploration have been a natural and not unexpected concomitant
of the system – rarely, so far as evidence is available and permits of a judgement, culminating in full sexual intercourse.
The school's policy has on the whole been a clear and consistent one – no sexual intercourse in term time and a sensitive

respect for and confidence in teenagers' own judgements in these matters, so long as they are contained within the framework of a full and satisfying programme of living and growing.

Lady Allen of Hurtwood (Bedales 1910) has remarked in her *Memoirs of an Uneducated Lady*: 'I believe that boys and girls from segregated schools are likely to be sent into the world, as E. M. Forster wrote in his notes on the English character, with well-developed bodies, fairly developed minds and under-developed hearts. At Bedales our hearts were certainly not under-developed.'

Esmond Romilly who, however, only spent eight weeks as a pupil at Bedales, refers to 'social sex of a lemonadish variety'.* An O.B. of the Forties writes:

As it *was* a boarding school, I think that for me the most important non-standard element was the presence of girls . . . Perhaps there was a contradiction in the Bedalian ethos: an assumption or naive hope that boys and girls brought up together in a healthy, well-aired environment, with lots of wholesome activity to occupy their minds and exercise their bodies, would just remain chums hardly aware of their potentially interesting differences.

Such an assumption might possibly once have been accurate; it has increasingly become less so in the post-war years.

A frequent reference in letters received from O.B.s of the Fifties and Sixties is to the strength of social cliques, of how some boys and girls were 'select' and others not, the distinction appearing to be based largely, though not entirely, on brains and a kind of sophistication flaunted by the former and denied to the latter. Such a phenomenon is especially striking because it contradicts earlier Bedalian conventions and presumably was reflecting similar, novel, discriminatory stratification in society at large. On the other hand a counteracting tendency also survived, namely the strong sense of kinship between all ages and generations of Bedalians.

Two other features of the mid-Fifties may also be indicative of changes in the general climate of the school. One was the cessation of the Chief's and Meier's camps, the other was the falling off in attendance at O.B. meetings. It seems as though

* *Out of Bounds*. London: Hamish Hamilton, 1937.

Bedalians were more and more beginning to find what they needed outside instead of inside the ambit of the school. Correspondence also reveals a considerable degree of self-consciousness regarding such matters as arrogance towards other kinds of schools, snobbery towards domestic staff and an over-ready inclination to take the easy way out available to the highly privileged. The single, most powerful feature however, which seems to mark the correspondence – and this is quite in line with the whole Bedalian tradition from the start – is the encouragement of non-conformity in thought and behaviour.

A girl pupil from the Fifties writes:

The essence for me was the social life, the extra-curricular activities. Bedales was like belonging to a huge family and gave us the opportunity of growing up in an atmosphere of friendship and benign experiences. The Fifties were not a sexually overt time and for most of us sexuality was not highly important. There were a few progressive types, but their activities and involvements were fairly secret. Most of us would now be regarded as having been inhibited, and we certainly were not exploding with curiosity when we left school. Pity really, it would be nice to be able to colour your book with tales which most people believe and hope are true about Bedalians. Falling in love was delightful, and the broken hearts and passions were just a small aspect of the social life. I remember the endless conversations most of all. I don't think I have ever met people so able to talk to each other. And the other thing one remembers, the smell of the art-room, the library, the plays and the merry evenings, the terrible dances and the self-conscious agony of growing up, and the Quad, and the Common Room, and how we hated games, and the clowns and the clevers and the hideous buildings and the beautiful idyllic countryside. And the record players in the dormitory and the cold baths (gone I hear) and seeing one's painting up in the dining room, and the good-night kisses and the rules we found to break. And I married a Bedalian and if he could be bothered to write down what he thought, he would remember different things. He loved games and his bicycle, and the printing works and smoking or getting up at night. He found far more rules to break than ever occurred to me, and he thought lessons unbelievably boring and time wasting, and that most of the teachers were either thick or vindictive. But he was happy. And really that too is the essence of Bedales. How we saw it, individually, and how it provided for us a chance to do what we wanted to do when we wanted to do it, and to find somebody who would do it with one. And the sorry part is that the whole of life isn't like that. I used to feel sorry for some of the wives or husbands of O.B.s when our friends began to get married. They found Bedalians very strange with their easy intimacy like a family of brothers and sisters; strange, confident girls who seemed to know their husbands (and vice versa) better than they did. Many a relationship crashed. And many a quarrel was started – I know because some of the wives were able to express it and found in the end that they could talk to Bedalians.

It is strange how undistinguished we all are. There are no great fighters, no climbers in society or strugglers to achieve. We are all too – what? It is probably complacent or smug?

This chapter can fittingly close with three more extracts from letters: the first two date from the mid-Sixties, the third from the Thirties. The first is from a boy pupil:

I think I shall be eternally grateful to Bedales for giving me the chance to discover talents for a whole variety of things that might have gone unnoticed at another school. People are still amazed if I tell them that in my 'A' Level year I had time to be in the school play, spend four hours a week in the Workshop, organise outdoor work, help run the boys' Flat, sing in the choir and still get some decent 'A' Levels. I enjoyed functioning in the very small community where one could see the effect of what one did and think that I have never been as purposeful as when I was at Bedales.

The second is from a girl pupil:

There were about 240 children and possibly 50 staff (that includes a large number of music teachers). This comprised an inner unit with an intense and somewhat insulated life of its own. If I start with the positive and unique (I believe, with some experience of other schools and systems to draw on) aspects of the place, I should list what this intimate network of close relationships (between staff and pupils, and between every individual there) gave to me, both personally and in a more definable educational sense.

It gave, and still gives, immense emotional stamina. Often a cruel place, for those not good-looking, intellectually able or confident, or gifted in some way, it made for an intensity of everyday experience that I think surpassed most extremes of adolescent development. A self-consciousness, an awareness of criticism, a very early responsiveness and knowledge of (not in the Biblical sense, despite publicity!) the opposite sex; these were the inevitable consequences of living a long day (from break-fast until assembly at 8.00 or 8.30 p.m.) and every weekend with the same group of people. Dormitories then were seldom fewer than five people to a room, and very Spartan by today's standards! This could lead to the forming of cliques, often of an exclusive, severely jealous kind – often on a basis known as being 'select'; to be branded 'un-select' could colour you for your whole school career (rather akin to U and Non-U although absolutely nothing to do with *Class*). But it worked in a subtle way to give a meaningful (not superficial) maturity of an emotional and psychological depth, that showed up immediately in the first year at University. Often it took the form of intellectual arrogance or superficial confidence; but I think a Bedalian of my generation, at least, could be picked out in a freshers' gathering immediately. Our immediate and supreme advantage was simply articulacy. This stemmed from a real maturity of thought and self-awareness, which, to me, is the main and most positive hallmark of the Bedales of my time. One had to learn quickly how to build up and defend a complex inner structure of self-protection. Reputa-tion certainly meant a great deal, and it was quickly hung about your neck and seldom modified in the light of different, better or worse behaviour. Our judgement of each other was not only of a moral kind (and those morals were not strictly of a Christian or accepted kind) but on the basis of ability and sensibility too. If you could keep your essential privacy at all times, then you were safe from the often savage character dismembering that was a common Bedalian pastime. This sounds rather uncivilised, but did have its strength-out-of-suffering aspects.

It also bore academic fruit. I don't think one had to be brilliant in order that the core of Bedalian intellectual education should implant itself in your life. That is: 'Think for yourself' as the unwritten motto. This was the encouragement, as a conscious teaching ethos, of the free and vigorous expression of thought. It taught a genuine curiosity of a profound kind, about people, history, literature and everything that matters. It meant one had, and has, opinions on everything, often not well informed, but always held with (sometimes aggressive) convictions. This, I find, is still against the common grain – where *attitudes* not opinions are more prevalent. To *know* what one thinks and feels and believes about nearly everything is, I am sure, a truly Bedalian characteristic; and the lasting achievement of convinced teaching.

It is difficult to assess or generalise concerning staff/children relationships, especially in retrospect. Inevitably one's adult vision re-focuses the experiences of being young, and only half-aware. But for the most part such relationships were open, honest and trustful. Certainly in the Sixth Form we were genuinely treated as equals – although I think it is to the eternal credit of the members of staff at that time that I, for one, never found such relationships over-familiar or without respect on both sides for the position of teacher and taught. The position of Housemaster or Housemistress was then the most influential and crucial, possibly their knowledge of and intrusion into the lives of individual children could have been described as unjustified. One knows now how easy it is to make snap judgements of character and then never to wish to re-open the case, as it were. The staff, too, were inextricably part of a ceaseless process of psychological investigation and analysis. We could never leave one another alone! These forces working in the daily life of the school were at their strongest when I was in the Sixth Form. Here relationships became more complicated, by longevity (many of my contemporaries at school had travelled up with me through Dunhurst) and by the sudden onslaught of worldly cares!

This is not a severe criticism; because in many ways Bedales would have been a duller place had it been more integrated into its time and environment, but certainly in the Sixties very little intruded from the political, industrial or educational world outside. I think we knew more of European culture at first-hand than of our contemporary society at home. The media for instance, now such a backcloth to our lives, seldom made an impression. We only saw television if royalty got married or died. I don't think we were allowed our own radios, and the occasional Rock

Group got seized upon for incessant playing in the Prefects'
Library [an initially unofficial, then official Sixth Form Common
Room]. This all added to our reliance upon articulate, passionate
and eloquent powers of self-expression through a single means of
communication, words – speech.

None of this made the transition from school to life outside at all easy. It meant and still means to many Bedalians that
making friends outside the school circle or leaving the place and
its people entirely behind was very difficult. The special features
of its unique (I would defend that) education made truly sophisticated, confident or quite definitely distinctive individuals out of
all of us. There were few dull Bedalians. Many arrogant, opinion-
ated, unkind ones, few immature or foolish ones. It was not a
place for the shy, the nervous or narrow-minded.

Finally, a former Head Boy reflects:

I suppose the strongest thing remaining with me after a lapse of
some forty years is a sense of the richness of the place, and I
mean this in no way pejoratively, though it extends to the
material side as well. I think we were the heirs of a great wealth
of non-conformist, liberal ideas that had their origin probably in
the ferment of the English revolution. We were of course quite
unaware of these origins, but we were not unaware of our
cultural riches and indeed of the fact that they had been handed
down to us. I became strangely aware (on rare occasions!) that
we were standing on men's shoulders. The very presence of
Ernest Gimson's architecture with its ancient native tradition
contributed to a powerful whole. In retrospect I believe that a
consciousness of this cultural heritage – its diversity and richness
– is the lasting gift that Bedales has for the nation. Music? Architecture? Natural relations between the sexes? (Whatever that
may mean!) In some ways it is easier to define the Bedales way
of life by identifying its genesis – perhaps genetics would be a
better word. The reaction against 19th century utilitarianism is an
obvious gene; the pre-Raphaelites, the aesthetic movement, social-
ism, liberal German philosophy are all visible in their influence.
There are, of course, many other converging streams that I haven't
the skill to identify, but the wealth of their genetic heritage is
undeniable and in a subtle way it was tangible at the time.

As for intellectual elements, this is a difficult one. How, for example, do you rate music? Is that intellectual or emotional? One of the most valuable elements in Bedalian education was a tacit understanding that purely intellectual qualities were not the be-all and end-all of life. What does the intellect know of beauty and love? What is the intellectual value of Keats' 'Ode to the Nightingale'? We live in a competitive, money-conscious world, but we don't only live in a competitive, money-conscious world, we live – perhaps more vividly – in other worlds as well. Bedales had to prepare its pupils to live effectively in the real world just as much as other schools; but it was in its attempt to acknowledge that reality had more than two dimensions – perhaps more than three – that Bedales shone irridescently. Yes, there is an intellectual component in this, and one can see its intellectual ancestry. But it is in its stress on the lasting value of things non-intellectual that it is significant. And this too is something all too rare in this last quarter of the 20th century.

ASSESSMENT

*

CHAPTER NINE

The Place of Bedales in Education

*

Because this is an unfinished story, it is too soon to offer more than a provisional estimate of the place of Bedales in education. An attempt to do so can be usefully preceded by an examination of the main criticisms which have been levelled against it. They are of three kinds, socio-political, educational and philosophical, and they have been made both by Bedalians themselves and non-Bedalians.

My principal criticism of Bedales, [writes an Old Boy of the mid-Fifties] is that it wished a social end without willing the means to attain it. The end was a co-operative society where collective development was not just opposed to but a necessary condition of individual development, where this development was seen not merely in material terms but in those of relationship, art, and the collective, non-authoritarian direction of the social course. Work of each for weal of all; a phrase offering a general social vision and reproduced on a micro-scale in the school itself. It was a vision which I recognised later when I read William Morris, particularly *News from Nowhere*. But Morris recognised that such a vision, to be socially realised, could only be preceded by a revolution. It could not be purchased with school fees. It required a political act and political organisation. Bedales, while rightly encouraging us to make universal claims for the values of the school, to extend the work of each for weal of all to all society, almost totally failed to point out the stakes involved. We were ignorant of the social conditions of the school's existence, of the material structures which produced the values and ways of living in later life which we had uneasily to face, of class experience and political

E

power in this country and internationally, which were the context for any genuine transition of a William Morris variety. This ignorance limited Bedales and Bedalians. Socially it was reflected in snobbery to pantry staff, Grammar school boys and girls, local inhabitants and so on. After school the cold air of capitalism blew many of us into depression, nostalgia, or back to individual versions of Cockshott Lane [a pleasant rural retreat near the school]. The microcosm could not be re-created, and most of us were totally unfitted for the more general project. Originally radicals within a ruling class, we remained trapped in that class, and the whole of Bedales' development has been increasingly to conform to the basic terms of that class, rather than to surpass and suppress it. In education the field of battle for the principles of Bedales has long since moved from the privileged ground of the Public School, and Bedales has failed to move with it. The root of the failure I would locate in the same general social and political insulation which has been the subject of this letter.

It is illuminating to lay alongside this quotation a passage from *Progressive Retreat; A sociological study of Dartington Hall School and some of its former pupils*: *

Our children of the new era have largely turned their backs on the burden of reforming that world which progressive education initially so strenuously denigrated. Rather, in the privacy of their own home or in the company of like-minded individuals, they can indulge in symbolic progressive rituals that stress social distance from the conventional middle class.

'Tap enough money boxes,' writes another Bedalian of the late Forties, 'and you can make a social island . . . Bedales teaches you to appreciate the good things of life without giving you any of the means to acquire them.'
An O.B. of the Sixties, writing from the U.S.A. remarks:

Bedales has a place in a class structure, that, seen from abroad, looks incredibly rigid, and it fulfils the demands placed on it in that structure admirably. Its method may be, and certainly was, progressive, but its purpose is not. The elitist feeling generated in the Bedalian is, from an academic point of view, not well justi-

* By Maurice Punch. Cambridge University Press, 1977. p. 143.

fied (in my experience). The feeling is, however, socially rather more appropriate. It is a matter of opinion whether a more democratic society is better, but I do not think that the 'progressive' rhetoric of Bedales should obscure its function, that of teaching scorn of what were openly called the 'proles', and support of the rather particular middle class values of what seemed in retrospect to have been a mostly professional class of parent.

'At the heart of Bedales,' writes a former member of staff, who later became headmaster of a large state secondary school, 'there was an unresolved paradox. The school was committed to reform of the existing social order but was itself a highly privileged establishment only existing because of the inequalities of wealth.'

Another O.B. of the early Forties writes:

As to the importance of the school, I would say that so far as education in Britain since the war is concerned, the whole history of Bedales is irrelevant, and the only reason the school is interesting at all is as an example of the activities of a particular class or a particular sub-culture during the first part of the century (on a par, say, with a Fabian Summer School or the Arts and Crafts Movement). Bedales nowadays, incidentally, seems to be nothing but an extremely expensive, highly privileged and prestigious enclave, and I can see no justification for interest in its existence at all!

One other contribution from a former Head Boy can quickly conclude the socio-political part of the criticisms:

All the school has proved so far is that Badley's principles can only be applied to a little hothouse community. Bedales today has *nothing* to offer our sick society. Despite exchanges with Comprehensives in Yorkshire and no doubt loads of other schemes to broaden everybody, Bedales remains completely out of touch with the pretty miserable lives that most members of an advanced industrial nation lead . . . I sometimes wonder what sort of school Badley might have thought of starting if he had been born a hundred years later and served his apprenticeship in a Comprehensive in Acton or Moss Side.

What does this socio-political criticism from within the school community amount to? Briefly, it is that a school originally conceived of as reformist, both of education and society, either did not or could not incorporate in its mode of conduct the necessary revolutionary ingredients for major social change. By not doing so, it was, furthermore, compelled to conform to the non-revolutionary, evolutionary and possibly even reactionary pressures of the wider society in which it was and is encapsulated. This simply points to a gigantic paradox in the Bedales story, namely, that the school started out as an innovatory, pioneering movement in a basically self-confident late Victorian society and became an assured, successful and established institution in a society which has become increasingly fragmented.

This leads on to the question posed by Robert Skidelsky in his article on Kurt Hahn (the German educationist associated with Salem School in Germany and Gordonstoun in Scotland) in *Encounter* (1961). 'Can education create or sustain a counter culture?' It looks as if the answer is: only so far as the culture already in existence is prepared to tolerate it. What then of the educational criticisms of Bedales? From within the community itself comes a noticeable, though not frequent, complaint by some O.B.s that not enough pressure was put on the gifted children to work up to their maximum capacity.

In a narrow, academic sense, the education as I remember it [writes an O.B. of the late Fifties] was soft. Considering that even at that time there was already a growing need to consider 'O's and 'A's there was little overt pressure to master a syllabus, particularly in the Arts subjects. (I have an idea that people who specialised in the Sciences had altogether a very different experience of Bedales?) Much emphasis was put on getting people to develop their own ideas, use the library themselves etc. This made me personally very unhappy; those hours of anxiety while one *didn't* read and write for one's history essay in the library – of writing poetry about a girl or discovering a new novelist instead of having even at that age to rationalise the value of these escapes. In retrospect I might well have been happier with firmer guidance.

Another O.B. pupil from the mid-Sixties provides an interesting counterpart:

In order to obtain two or more 'A' Levels I spent my final year of schooling at Maidstone Grammar School. I did not find much difference between myself and comparable pupils in that school; so, although Bedales was good, I would not have preferred it necessarily to a Grammar School of those days. Interestingly, I did not find that Bedales' education in academic terms was more progressive than at Maidstone: the ideas taught, in History for example, were similar and the texts sometimes identical.

The next long quotation is worth pondering even though the writer of it, an O.B. of the Forties, does not seem wholly convincing or successful in his argument.

I was a Prefect for my last two years and Head Boy for my last term. I was extremely happy at the school and I think fairly successful socially. At the time I believed it to be one of the best schools in the country and certainly one of the most significant and progressive – and my impression is that this view was shared by most other people connected with it. Within a few years of leaving, though, I realised that this was quite wrong, and that really there was a kind of dishonesty about the culture of Bedales (culture in an anthropological sense) – indeed there was something unhealthy and unnatural about it: I no longer felt it should be counted as an enlightened or progressive school at all. I accept, obviously, that it was decent, tolerant, friendly, informal, liberal, with a fairly artistic and intellectual atmosphere (as schools go), and there was very little fear, bullying or homesickness. But these qualities didn't preclude the unhealthiness I have come to recognise – and this fact now seems to me the most interesting thing about it, for it indicates the weakness in otherwise impressive educational theories. The trouble I think derived from the need (as it was thought) to maintain social order – and how this need was fulfilled. As you know, the boast was that there was no formal system of discipline in the school: if there had to be punishments, they wouldn't be frightening or pointless as in the traditional Public School, but devised to fit the crime and fit the criminal; normally, though, it was thought, discussion and reason would suffice (even clubs have to have rules . . . what would happen if everyone did it? etc.) This was the myth rather than an accurate picture of our experience, but I am not concerned with practical short-comings: the point I want to make is about how the system worked at its best, or as well as could reasonably be expected, and what the price of *that* was, for I think the unhealthiness was built into the system: in ideal circumstances it wouldn't have occurred, but in normal circumstances it was bound to.

What was encouraged was called 'self-discipline', as opposed to imposed discipline; but what this actually meant was that we were kept in order by means of personal relationship – it wasn't *really* self-discipline, for we did what we were told, and what was expected of us, in order to earn the good opinion of members of the staff and the good opinion of older children: we wanted to be trusted, respected, thought mature and given responsibilities; we were bribed with prestige and status. Of course, on the face of it, getting children to behave well so as to earn the esteem of sensible people sounds an excellent way to run a school (after all, it's close to what happens in a family), but it didn't work *naturally*, in reality it was more like a confidence trick – for if the system was to work, being respected by members of the staff, having a personal relationship with them, getting on up the hierarchy of the school, and so on, had not just to be valued, but over-valued. And thus was cooked up a degree of seriousness and self-consciousness in the school, priggishness is really the word for it, and a smugness which for a long time I found embarrassing to recollect! The school encouraged holiness, pseudery and posing in children and in staff. Incidentally I think a lot of the social control achieved by the older children was by means of a sort of patron/client relationship they would have with younger children. Such relationships were often the result of having been in the same dormitory. The strength of a prefect depended on the number and influence of his clients. This was an informal and unverbalised system.

I know of course that many of these things happen in other schools too, particularly boarding schools (I mean, that they come to be taken over-seriously), but Bedales seems to have been worse than most, a veritable hothouse for the growth of this corruption. That's what I mean by the price exacted by the system of social control, for it was worse *because* of the principles on which it was run when run by normal people. I certainly wouldn't advocate authoritarian discipline instead, but at least a school run in that way breeds a kind of counter-culture, the staff aren't unnaturally admired: they don't need to have that kind of intense relationship, as they have other sanctions than withdrawal of favour. At Bedales though, there was no tradition of cultural revolt, no natural rejection of establishment values and attitudes (which in my day were very élitist). And it's surely revealing (and depressing) that people seem to remain Bedalians even more than people remain Etonians or Wellingtonians, but it's not surprising: it was a school that was bound to induce just this kind of immaturity. What I have been talking about, I suppose, is an aspect of the truth behind one of Bedales' main claims to be enlightened and progressive – namely the close relationship between staff and children there. That there are boys and girls together in boarding school is or was Bedales' other main claim to enlightenment and progressiveness. This was in fact less healthy and natural than it might have been, and seeing why this was so provides a significant illustration of precisely what I think wrong with the school, i.e. it shows one consequence of this need for a cooked-up mutual admiration society.

With the tacit encouragement of the staff, boys generally accepted the belief that a full sexual relationship was something that would come later, after school, as part of a loving marriage: it wasn't fitting or suitable at school when we were, after all, only seventeen or eighteen! And girls, the kind of girls that went to Bedales, at any rate, it was thought, didn't experience orgasm; their enjoyment of sex was mild and could only be part of a loving relationship; and they would not initiate sex, or be demonstrative; sex was something they might 'let boys do', but if they were positively sexual, it would be rather shocking. I am not quoting my opinion particularly, nor claiming that this is what every boy would have necessarily believed entirely; I am trying to guess at a sort of consensus. The result was that when one headmaster, for instance, went round classrooms just before bedtime to rout out couples who were kissing good-night, it wasn't considered an outrageous intrusion, nor was the after-dark rule which forbade boys to leave the building after dark. I don't mean that these rules were faithfully obeyed necessarily, but they were more or less accepted as a reasonable position, the line the

school was right to take. It was generally agreed in fact that
it would be wrong for sex to go 'too far', and the boys' idea
of 'too far' wouldn't have been all that different from the
authorities'.

This compromising, hedging, hoping that where the line was
drawn would be respected, sort of attitude towards sex was
there I think ever since girls had first been admitted; and it isn't
surprising, given the period and social class – I am certainly not
blaming anyone! But at Bedales, with the situation I've described, these notions were particularly unfortunate because, of
course, inevitably, there was no revolt against them – the establishment had too much prestige, it seemed so reasonable and
civilised. At ordinary schools at the time the children would
also have heard this same rubbish about sex from their elders,
but there would have been more scepticism, more of a counter-
culture, there would have been other sources of information, it
wouldn't have been all accepted as part of a package, with the
result they would have had more genuine freedom to experiment.
And this illustrates precisely my criticism about Bedales : there
was a myth of freedom, but so far from being free we were in
truth being indoctrinated extremely efficiently by an insidious
culture. This, arguably, wouldn't have mattered had the culture
been entirely admirable, but as I have said before, you can't set
up an educational system expecting the ideal. How damaging it
in fact was is too difficult to say; it is revealing though that
Bedalians of that generation, contrary I am sure to theoretical
expectation, do not seem since to have been conspicuously successful in sexual or emotional relationships (this is my impression at any rate). All schools were and are pretty awful places,
and I dare say Bedales was no worse than a lot of others,
obviously it wasn't : but the point I'm making is, it wasn't much
better either, better that is at producing intellectually and emotionally mature people, and this is exactly what it should have
been if it was to claim convincingly that it was significant and
progressive.

To conclude this glance at educational criticism of Bedales,
it is enlightening to consider the following judgement of Professor A. C. Stewart on what may be considered 'progressive' :

Perhaps at the end we may now have to say that what has been called progressive in relation to the world between 1750 and 1970 no longer signifies. To meet a new challenge of size, mechanisation, rationalised man, and the transformation of work and leisure, a different kind of progressive school must arise to correct the social and economic inequalities which history has provided, and to take opportunity by the forelock. Here large, comprehensive schools are tending to become the norm and mechanical aids the necessary supplement to teachers. The simulations of mental processes which have been applied in programmed instruction and the computer provide a new dimension and may enforce a re-evaluation of the school as a social community. Here the notion of the school as an extended family is not only not progressive any more, it may be an anachronism. (op. cit., p. 484.)

Turning now to the third line of criticism, namely a philosophical one, a good start is the following passage from Jacques Maritain's *Education at the Crossroads*.*

Modern pedagogy has made invaluable progress in stressing the necessity of carefully analysing and fixing its gaze on the human subject. The wrong begins when the object to be taught and the primacy of the object are forgotten, and when the cult of the means – not to an end but without an end – only ends up in a psychological worship of the subject.

How far has Bedales yielded to that temptation of progressive education? In its origins and early days, hardly at all, for while concentration on 'the human subject' was intense, the end was, if only implicitly, always there: it was personified in the character of Badley and his ethical Christianity of a non-symbolic kind, severely practical and strongly tinged with a faith in social meliorism. Now, while such an attitude was potent and extended outwards from Bedales and lasted on into the Thirties, it suffered from one serious metaphysical defect. It failed to discriminate between good and God, between mistake and sin, between maladjustment and evil, between putting up with life and coming to terms with death. The poverty of its metaphysics began to show up under the

* New Haven, Conn.: Yale University Press, 1943. p. 14.

E*

cruel spotlights of totalitarianism, the Second World War, the Cold War and the violence-spawning aridity of the Fifties and the Sixties. Writing in *The Observer* of 30 November 1975 on Solzhenitsyn's *Gulag Archipelago* Volume II, William Crankshaw remarked: 'For a number of generations Western man had lost the sense of evil. Faced with manifestations that were clearly evil, his instinct was to treat them as aberrations. But, now, we know that evil can be everywhere at once.'

The philosophical criticism that may be levelled against Bedales is that, once the implicit end of the Badley era disappeared, no other end took its place, and so pupils at Bedales failed to be educated in a sense of evil as distinct from a mere awareness of social misfit or personal misfortune. That there was some appreciation of this lack is shown by the fact that in the Fifties, Sixties and Seventies occasional attempts were made to introduce a specifically Christian orientation into the school, but these did not succeed, and so the only ends overtly recognized were increasingly those of academic success and the attainment of human happiness, neither of them buttressed by any educational teleology.

Attention having been drawn to at least three possible warts, socio-political, educational and philosophical, on the face of Bedales, it is right and proper to put finishing touches to our picture by summarizing the positive and impressive aspects of the school's achievements. However, in so doing, it is imperative to remember the undoubted fact that education is always more the resultant than the determinant of human affairs, even while granting that the resultant itself is one of the determinants of subsequent human developments. This point is well made in a letter received from an O.B.:

My belief is that the years have produced a fine school but that its contribution to the development of education and questioning of educational principles ceased in, say, 1950. What would be particularly interesting to identify is how far what happened at Bedales up to 1950 was in a sense in a self-contained compartment merely reflecting general progressive, philosophical ideas, or whether the visible success of Bedales in co-education, in methods of teaching, in the comprehensive range and level of subjects taught and in the general non-authoritarian character of the school with few rewards or penalties, gave clear impetus to the extension of that form of education in other schools, including the State sector.

In responding to that challenge, the proposition will here be advanced that impetus has undoubtedly been given to the extension of the Bedalian form of education in other schools, including the state sector.

Beyond argument, the strongest influence of Bedales in education has been exercised through the character of its founder, although, as must have become clear, many other influences than those of that outstanding individual have been at work.

When I had been at Bedales about ten years, [writes Geoffrey Crump]. I said to O. B. Powell one day, 'You know it's a curious thing that I have been here ten years and have had many conversations with Badley, but not one, that I remember, on any subject but Bedales and education.' And O. B. P., who had been at Cambridge with Badley and was one of his closest friends, replied, 'But neither have I!'

As Mr Badley turned into the Chief, personal history became collective myth. While it is essential to distinguish between the two, what Bedales has become is the product of their merging and even, it could be argued, their confusion. In a letter addressed to Badley in 1965, the master of Trinity College Cambridge (then Lord Adrian) wrote as follows:

At a meeting of the Council of Trinity College on January 28th it was agreed that I should send you our best wishes on your 100th Birthday. We are extremely proud to be reminded that Bedales School was founded by a Scholar of the College, and we are delighted to think that seventy-two years later he is able to see the general acceptance of the principles which he did so much to establish.

On the same occasion Badley received the following tribute from the Mayor of Dudley:

We in Dudley take much pride in your long and distinguished career in education – a career in which at a very early stage, you made your mark by becoming in fact, the effective Founder of co-education in Britain and this, I believe, has had too a very great influence on Secondary education generally.

Both these passages are referring to that change in educational climate of Western society brought about by such pioneers as Badley himself, Reddie of Abbotsholme, Paul Geheeb of the Odenwaldschule and L'Ecole d'Humanité, A. S. Neill of Summerhill, Kurt Hahn of Salem, W. B. Curry of Dartington Hall, George Lyward of Finchden Manor and others both in Europe and the U.S.A. These do not constitute a homogeneous group, and their outlooks swing between the benevolently paternalistic and the anarchistically permissive, with an ideology always left of centre, but itself ranging within that compass from right to left. Badley himself belonged to the right wing of that left of centre.

Introduction of the word myth is deliberate: it is used to denote what, while originating in Badley the individual, has transcended him, namely such Bedalian outlooks and attitudes which have largely unconsciously permeated most educational reform. It is the myth, both true and false, of the perfectibility of man by means of appropriate up-bringing. The criteria of appropriateness can obviously receive different interpretations at various stages of the school's history, but the essence of the myth has remained constant; that is, the legitimacy and virtue of individual aspiration to self-fulfilment and the assumption that this in itself is a sufficient guarantee of a sound social ethic and a coherent philosophy. In Badley himself it surely was: the best witness to that is the manner in which, nearly fifty years after his retirement, his spirit can still be sensed in the school – the feeling that the great man has lived there among his staff and his pupils and has not laboured in vain to make possible what his successors have managed to preserve and develop.

This influence could best be summed up as the humanization of boarding-school life. The following is an institutional acknowledgement of it:

July 1935

We, the undersigned Heads of co-educational schools, ask you to accept the small gift of a Persian rug in token of the admiration which we feel for your service to the cause of co-education and in acknowledgment of the inspiration and encouragement which your work at Bedales has afforded to us all.
Signed :

Ernest Barratt – Dursley Secondary School
Olive M. Bidwell – Halstead Place School
M. S. Brooks – The Hall School, Weybridge
Cyril and Jean Cator – Alcester Grammar School
Margaret Clutten – Homer Farm School
W. B. Curry – Dartington Hall
A. M. Dell – County House School, Braintree
Walter Dobbie – South Downs School, Steyning
Edward and Elisabeth Dorman – The Lawns School, St Austell
Cecile Dunham and Louise Laity – Ingomar School, Walton-on-Thames
Anna Essinger – New Herrlingen, Bunce Court, Otterden
A. E. Filsell – Lady Manners School, Bakewell
Basil A. Fletcher – Chippenham School, Wiltshire
C. B. Furneaux – Aylesbury Grammar School
Paul Geheeb – Odenwaldschule
W. A. Grace – Halesowen Grammar School, Birmingham
Cecil Grant – St George's School, Harpenden
D. Gurney – Roydes Hall School, Huddersfield
The College of Teachers of the New School, Streatham Hill
H. Lyn Paris and Eleanor A. Paris – St Christopher's, Letchworth
A. E. Harrison – Ecclesfield Grammar School, Sheffield
A. T. L. Hickson – Oldfield, Swanage
Basil A. Howard – Addey & Stanhope School
H. Howe – Keswick School
J. L. Howson – Bicester County School
Hyatt and Birkett – King Alfred School
Grace Littleboy – Friends School, Saffron Walden
Dorothy Matthew – St. George's Children's House, Harpenden

John R. Morrison – Cornarghmore Higher Grade School, Scarinish, Isle of Tiree

A. S. Neill – Summerhill School, Leyston

F. L. Nordern – Cockburn High School, Leeds

Frank Oldham – Hincksea Grammar School, Leicestershire

W. N. Palmer – Sidcot School

F. W. Payne – Rochdale Secondary School

Margaret B. Reed and J. E. Lovett – Pinehurst School, Heathfield

Paul Roberts – Frensham Heights School

Frank Sandon – Plymouth Corporation Grammar School

Annie Smith – Eastleigh County High School

G. R. Swaine – Kingsmore School, Glossop

C. L. Tompson and V. C. Watson – St. Bride's School, Hove

A. R. M. Trenter – Queen Elizabeth Grammar School, Penrith

C. E. Vernon – Southall County School

S. Wilkinson – Grammar School, Letchworth

E. Joy Wragg – The High School, Welwyn Garden City

The headmaster of the Friends School, Great Ayton, North Yorkshire, wrote in 1965 to Badley:

We in the Quaker Schools have always greatly admired Bedales and felt that it achieved much that we failed to embody in our schools. We are indebted to many of the ideas which you put into practice, and we have always recognised Bedales as a pioneer, but we were quietly practising co-education for the greater part of last century and in this we were I think ahead of our time, though we did tend to be rather more narrow-minded in some other respects.

The Headmaster of Waterford School, Swaziland, wrote to Badley in 1964:

Last week I drove to Johannesburg to meet two girls who left school last year. On their own initiative they arranged to come out here for a term to help us at our small new multi-racial, multi-denominational, multi-faith boys' boarding secondary school, which we started last year in this tiny backwater of a contracting Commonwealth. They are already helping magnificently. It is no accident that these girls should come from the school you founded. We now have contact with many places in England, but none provides a warmer link, more sympathy or greater interest than Bedales. The KIT [Keep in Touch] committee's contribution, the exchange of letters and drawings and the arrival of these two girls all prove this. In one sense Waterford is part product of the short but enjoyably stimulating time I spent on the staff in 1949 and 1950, because I found at Bedales a deep humanity cutting across all man-made barriers of race and religion. This is what is needed all over the world, but especially in South Africa, and that is why Waterford, broadly based on a Christian foundation, has opened its doors to boys of all colours and creeds. I think you would approve.

The Saffron Walden Parent/Teacher Association wrote to Badley in 1965: 'We send our thanks, because the idea which you had the courage to initiate has flourished, not least in this school. We owe much to you, and we know it.'

In the teasing task of trying to assess influence, the following contribution from an O.B. is a helpful one:

The example of Badley, Bedales, Bedales staff and, to a lesser extent, Old Bedalians, has undoubtedly had a tremendous effect; firstly on comparable schools (what Skidelsky calls the 'incestuous merry-go-round') King Alfred's, Dartington, Monkton Wild etc. Secondly, on schools that did not, indeed do not, consider themselves to be progressive. (Who can define that term?) Badley has often been described as a pioneer. That gives no indication of his incredible and complete conception of Bedales life nor of the success and influence of it. I wonder if 'visionary' is the more accurate word – perhaps 'visionary pioneer'? It is not insignificant that the advent of the New Education Fellowship did not sway him from his course despite their aims over-lapping in certain areas – his North country doggedness paid off handsomely.

An integral part of the humanization of boarding-school life was of course co-education: in spite of occasional complaints by old pupils about what they suffered as a consequence of having to come to terms with inter-sex relationships in adolescence and the poor preparation it gave some of them for marriage, the evidence of its beneficial effect is impressive, and it comes from all generations. Although three stages of development may be detected in the pattern of girl/boy relationship – good chum–sibling up to the mid-Twenties; romantic–experimental up to the Forties; and the much more permissive one since then, all these largely reflecting the habits of society outside – certain merits of Bedalian co-education remain constant. First, there is the purely practical one of knowledge of one sex of its opposite through daily encounter in classroom and Quad; second, there is the emotional and intellectual stimulus of learning side by side in different ways about the same subject, more particularly in an aesthetic sense; third, there is the immensely valuable realization that girls and boys are persons far more than mere sex objects.

Probably the most direct evidence concerning the effect of co-educational practice at Bedales on the outside world is provided by Dr L. R. Wood:

Bedales converted me to co-education. When I was shortlisted for the post of headmaster at Brockenhurst I discovered from the other candidates that the Local Education Authority proposed to split the school which was growing very rapidly, the boys remaining in the present building, the girls moving to a new school on a 12-acre site at the other end of Brockenhurst. I was offered the post but declined it on the ground that I believed in co-education and was totally opposed to their development plan.

However, I was persuaded by the Director and Chairman to accept the post on their assurance that it was only a plan and could be amended and on these assurances I came to Brockenhurst. Two years later the Chairman of the Education Committee met parents, including those who had recently transferred their boys and girls from one-sex schools, and found overwhelming support from parents and staff for the retention of co-education. As a result the school was not split, another co-ed Grammar School was built at Totton and eight years later a third erected at High Cliff. Today the whole of the New Forest area is staunchly co-educational. Parents demanding segregated schools have to search for them at Southampton or Bournemouth.

It is only possible to give a few examples of the way in which Bedales has influenced men and women who, after being on the staff, went on to work in other fields of education. A former Director of Education for Staffordshire County Council wrote to Badley, in 1964:

It is thirty-four years since I left Bedales to take up a lectureship in education at University College, Exeter, but my memories of the school remain as fresh as ever, for I loved every minute of my time there. It was a great thrill to be appointed Geography master to the school I had read and heard so much about, and, although professionally I may now have progressed, I have never again been so happy as I was at Petersfield. Those were formative years in my career, allowing the boast of having taught at Bedales under its Founder. How readily there floods to mind the personalities who served you then – Osbos, genial and kindly; Gimmy, cautious and meticulous; the exotic Gi-gi; Geoffrey Crump, serious yet humorous, to mention a few. Pip Smithells was Head Boy, and there were the Hale twins, my doughty opponents at Fives. You gave me 4A to master with such members as Johnny Brook and Marjorie Brown and quiet, unassuming Harman, who gave me coins and stamps of Lundy Island, his father's kingdom. I prize them still in memory of the boy who posthumously won the V.C. in World War II.

If space would allow I should want to reminisce and ramble on, to remind you of when you allowed me to introduce the then novel intelligence test technique within the school – the experiments in teaching Geography I carried out, but chiefly the talks I had with you in the study or on the lawn about education and philosophy. I expect you have forgotten that you presented me with an autographed copy of *The Will to Fuller Life* [a philosophical and psychological work by Badley] which is at hand as I write these lines. I left the University service in 1934 to become Deputy Director of Education for Middlesbrough, and two years later came to Staffordshire as Deputy, following F. A. Hughes who was formerly on the Bedalian staff, and then as Director in 1947.

A former member of Bedales staff, who went on to become headmistress of Sidcot School in Somerset and then of a large High School for girls – all African – in Kenya, comments:

I came to Bedales in May 1936 while I was doing my teaching practice at the Institute of Education in London – it was Sir

Percy Nunn's last year. For a very inexperienced teacher – background the Mount School and Westfield College – Bedales was all rather heady stuff. Though I humped a large number of books to Dunhurst I didn't do justice to the academic demand of such a job, and I've always regretted that. However, I have always been glad of my Bedales experience.

Another former member of staff, having become headmaster of a large Comprehensive School, writes:

I recognise that the name of Bedales still exercises considerable influence and arouses admiration, so that my own subsequent history would have been very different probably if the Governors and L.E.A. advisers had not thought that experience at Bedales was a very positive recommendation . . . As a result of experience in Comprehensive schools, the short-comings of an education system divided into a maintained and an independent sector have assumed increasing importance in my mind. Perhaps inevitably the very merits of Bedales become grounds of criticism in that they symbolise inequality of opportunity which the divided system perpetuates.

Dr R. S. Pease, Director of Culham Laboratory (United Kingdom Atomic Energy Authority), writes:

Roughly speaking, work of each for weal of all and other egalitarian, non-doctrinal outlooks inculcated at Bedales have in fact been of great value in keeping one's feet in the managerial revolution of the last twenty years. When one encounters this Bedalian pragmatic humanism, it can shine like a beacon in a morass of prejudice and misunderstanding.

The following letter may be allowed to speak for large numbers of O.B.s whose bodily and spiritual health was enriched by their time at Bedales. It is from Marianne Pospielowsky (Dunhurst 1910–12: Bedales 1912–14), a Russian:

A Letter to the Free People from a Displaced Person (1947)

I had the great privilege to be at Bedales School in my childhood. Unfortunately I could not stay long, for in 1914, during the summer holidays, when I was at home in Russia, the First World War began, and it was impossible to get to England. But during those four and a half years that I spent at Bedales a great amount of bodily and spiritual health was given to me . . . how grateful I always felt to this ideal school which gave me strength to stand all that I have had to suffer.

What then has this study of Bedales revealed? First, that the original objective of its founding, namely the limited one of correcting through example some of the defects of the Public School system, has been attained. Within the privileged context of Independent School education it has shown how a humane, co-educational boarding-school life can flourish without the sanctions of fear or the spur of individual competitiveness. Second, Bedales has exercised a modest influence on the public sector of education in two ways, partly by offering itself as a working educational model of which educationists of widely divergent views have taken notice and from which they have taken whatever suited their own purposes, and partly by providing opportunities for many young teachers to try out their own ideas in practice before proceeding to hold responsible positions themselves in administration and teaching elsewhere. Third, the study has demonstrated in the person of J. H. Badley how one man's vision, genius and determination can not only initiate educational change but also provide the impetus for his successors to safeguard and develop it. Fourth, and this may well be the best justification of its existence, especially in the eyes of those who criticize it on ideological grounds, Bedales has become an eloquent witness to a certain and most precious kind of freedom. Namely, for staff and pupils to ask any question in heaven or earth, however strange or unorthodox, and to respect any answer to it which is given in good faith, irrespective of whether the question proceeds from a scruffy young boy, a sophisticated maiden, or indeed from any honestly enquiring member of staff. In Ibsen's *The Wild Duck*, so much beloved by the Chief, there was a special loft for those cursed or honoured with the thirst for something more: true Bedalians are in that sense for ever thirsty – their education has made them so.

Useful References

★

1. The Bedales Archives in the school library contain past numbers of the *Bedales Record* (*B.R.*) and the *Bedales Chronicle* (*B.C.*) – the former an official account, the latter an informal continuing commentary and news sheet.
2. The *Bedales Roll* (periodically published; latest edn. 1978) contains biographical information about former Bedalian pupils and staff and some interesting statistics concerning careers and marriages.
3. *John Haden Badley 1865–1967. Bedales School and its Founder.* Editors: Gyles Brandreth and Sally Henry. Published by the Bedales Society, 1967.
4. *Bedales 1935–1965. Memories and Reflections.* 1978. A collection of essays compiled for domestic circulation.

Constitution

★

Bedales School is an Educational Charity recognised both by the Ministry of Education and by the Inland Revenue. As a charity it is exempt from income tax. This enables it to recover tax on investment and endowment income, and upon donations under Deeds of Covenant from which much of its capital development has been financed. Its constitution is in a modern form being that of a Company limited by Guarantee, not having a share capital. Owing to its status as a charity it is permitted by the Board of Trade to omit the word 'Limited' from its title, but in all other respects it is governed by the provisions of the Companies Act of 1948.

The objects of the School are set out in its Memorandum and the conduct of its affairs in the Articles of Association. These are revised when necessary so that the School's management need never be hampered by obsolete restrictions. Under these Articles the powers and duties of the Headmaster are set out in general terms worded in such a way as to allow him, as far as is consistent with the objects of the School, wide freedom to apply his own influence and ideas to the School and its development.

The Company consists of not more than one hundred members who themselves nominate new Members to fill vacant places. A stated number of places must be filled by Old Bedalians together with a member of the Teaching Staff. Members retire in groups by rotation every eight years but are eligible for re-election. They are responsible for the continuity of the School as a legal body, working within its Memorandum and Articles, and as such they are kept informed of the general progress of the School, and inspect and pass the accounts. It is also their duty to elect from their number a Board of Governors not exceeding twelve. The Governors are responsible for the appointment of the Headmaster, the general supervision of the educational affairs of the school, its policy, future development and finances. They serve for a maximum of eight years subject to interim retirement by rotation. It is to the Governors that Her Majesty's Inspectors of Schools make their reports after their periodic visits.

APPENDIX III

Numbers in School

		1936/7			1946/7			1956/7			1966/7			1976/7		
		B.	G.	Total	B.	G.	Total	B.	G.	Total	B.	G.	Total	B.	G.	Total
Bedales	Boarders	86	69	155	84	93	177	103	100	203	110	111	221	142	154	296
	Day	6	7	13	6	7	13	9	17	26	8	13	21	39	30	69
Middle School	Boarders	—	—	—	—	—	—	—	—	—	—	—	—	30	31	61
	Day	—	—	—	—	—	—	—	—	—	—	—	—	11	19	30
Dunhurst	Boarders	24	25	49	30	25	55	40	32	72	41	40	81	11	11	22
	Day	9	14	23	10	16	26	18	19	37	22	16	38	24	25	49
Dunannie	Day	—	—	—	—	—	—	10	20	30	18	20	38	22	20	42
TOTAL				240			271			368			399			569
Sixth Formers included in above		6	2	8	20	18	38	28	25	53	35	35	70	69	72	141

The total number of pupils who have passed through the school since 1893 is over 4,000

Index

★

Abbotsholme, 18, 19
Allen of Hurtwood, Lady, 57, 119

Badley, J. H.:
  the 'Chief', 31
  characteristics of, 15, 21, 71, 76, 78
  the man and the myth, 139–40
Barker ('Biff'), 59, 108
Barnes, K. C. B., ('Banner'), 71, 114
Barnsley, Edward, 108
Bedales School:
  aims of, 1–2
  Boys' Flat, 117
  Constitution of, 150
  criticisms of, 56, 63, 121–4, 129–38
  entrance tests, 90
  first prospectus, 20
  games, 110
  Girls' Flat, 117
  Grant Trust Fund, 90
  hallmark, 109
  impression of, in 1900, 28–9
  inspections of, 68, 98
  manifesto of 1900, 31–2
  numbers of pupils, 152
  pioneering role of, 34
  recognition by Board of Education, 33
  re-organization in 1960s, 95–6
  reputation abroad, 29–30, 35
  self-government, 57, 117–18
Bennett, H. E. W., ('Benn'), 110
Biggs, Ronald, 107, 111

Caiger-Smith, Joyce, 94
camps, 66–8
Carpenter, Edward, 17, 18
Cash, Christopher, 109
Child, Hu and Lois, 71
Clarke, Amy, 101
Cobb, Winifred (Mrs Powell), 22, 23
co-education, 25–6, 36, 46–8, 73, 93, 118–19, 143–4
Cormack, Miss ('Cor'), 100–104

Crump, Barbara, 115
Crump, Geoffrey, 54–6, 66

Dalton System, 59–60
Dickinson, 'Goldie' Lowes, 16–17, 24, 27, 58
drama:
  the Chief's productions, 48–50, 61–2
  in general, 112–14
Dunhurst, 100–106
Dunannie, 104–5
Durrell, Nommie, 109

Eckersley, Peter, 37

Field, Rachel Carey, 112–13
Fish, Mrs S. C., 101–2
Fry, Roger, 16, 27

Gardiner, Rolf, 65
Garrett, Amy, ('Ma B'), 16
Garrett, Edmund, 16, 27
Garstang, T. J., 22, 38
Gimson, Basil, ('Gimmy'), 35, 58–9, 77
Grant-Watson, E. L., 37–8, 59
'Great Debate' (1970), 19

handshaking, 35
Hobbs, Miss Irene, 62, 86, 88
Hogg, Stephen, 104
Horsley Laboratories, 54

Jacks, H. B., 83, 90
Jarman, Bill, 91
'Jaws' (Sunday evening addresses), 116–17
Jukes, Douglas, 104

King, Cyril, 94
King, Joan, (née Burnham), 115

Langlands, Alastair, 104–5
Library, 54, 115

Lupton, G. H., 31
Lupton Hall, 35

MacDonald, Malcolm, 51, 65, 69
MacDonald, Ramsay, 39, 69
Marshall, Alfred, H.M.I., 37
Meier, F. A., 67, 83–4, 87, 88–9
Meier, Mrs Sheena, 85–6
Meo, Innes, ('Gi-Gi'), 66, 109–10
Meredith, George, 39
Merry Evenings, 26, 40
Messingham, ('Chips'), 103–4
Messingham, Mary, (née Cocker), 103–4
Middle School, 104
motto, of school, 27
music, 111–12

New Education Fellowship, (now World Education Fellowship), 56, 58, 75
Nobes, C. Patrick, 83, 98

Old Bedalians:
  meetings of, 35, 39, 42
  Club, 51
outdoor work, 108

Pearson, G., 104–5
Pease, Dr R. S., 146

Powell, O. B., ('Osbos'), 22, 23, 24, 58
Powell, Roger, 108–9
Progressive School Movement, 15, 38, 75, 137
Public School system, 11, 16, 19, 20–1

Quad, the, 31, 46, 61, 114

Reddie, Cecil, 17, 18, 24
religion, 45, 92
Rice, Charles, 22
Roper, R. E., 50–1, 62
Rothenstein, Sir John, 53

siesta, 35
Slack, T. W., 83, 94
Steephurst, 31
Stocks, Mrs, 20
Studio, the, 109–10
Suffragettes, 17, 38

Tagore, Rabindranath, 115–16
Tatchell, Sophie, 104
Townsend, Paul, 104

Walesby, Jack, 91
Wood, L. R., 87–8, 144
Workshop, the, 108–9

Zilliacus, Laurin, 56